A Fly on the Garden Wall
(Or the Adventures of a Mobile Gardener)

By Michael K Chapman

A Fly on the Garden Wall.

Stories based on the Adventures of an inexperienced and somewhat foolhardy mobile landscape gardener learning by trowel and error the mysterious ways of horticulture and botany. Follow the humorous mishaps, minor disasters and strange but funny experiences of a hapless would be gardener as he attempts to make his way to profit and fortune while tackling menacing hordes of vicious brambles, murderous trees and shrubs, wicked weeds and eccentric customers.

A Fly on the Garden Wall
(Or the Adventures of a Mobile Gardener)

Other titles by this author.

The Fly series: A Fly on the Ward

Non-fiction: Humanology

Table of Contents.

Chapter One: First customer.

Filled with excitement and some trepidation I manhandled the old lawn mower on to my old car trailer and lashed it down with a length of nylon rope I had found the day before, I was like a boy scout, well prepared. I was waiting for my friend and new business partner to consume his sixth cup of tea and third cigarette - his normal breakfast, before joining me on the very first day of our business enterprise. We had both been unemployed for some time and little chance of employment loamed on our horizon. Totally fed up with no job, no money and no prospects for the future, we determined we would become millionaires. Giving the matter some moments thought over a few pints of beer, we decided to enter the world of self employment and start our own business. As neither of us had much experience or skills or even much intelligence for that matter, we decided upon a cunning plan.

Over the previous couple of days I had driven around my local area in an attempt to discover a niche in the employment market that would eventually bring us riches. The only things I saw in my meanderings were numerous unkempt gardens and uncut lawns and

then the Eureka moment struck. We would become
mobile gardeners! The result of my dastardly plan was
to offer our services to all who could not tend their own
gardens, those who did not wish to tend their gardens
and those who had long since forgotten they even had a
garden.

The idea was so simple it could not fail. There
was no initial large financial outlay apart from fuel for
my car and the mower, very opportune as neither of us
had more than pennies between us. I was the proud
owner of a beat up motor vehicle and a self built box
trailer. My business partner owned an old Suffolk
Punch lawnmower that had certainly seen better days,
and while he had some horticultural knowledge, I had
none. A good start but I was unconcerned. Between us
we managed to gather an odd assortment of gardening
implements, all uniform in colour: the colour of rust. A
few more beers and we had formulated a business plan,
sort of. We had worked out a price to charge by the hour
and set ourselves a target, we would work reasonable
hard, neither of us wanted to over do things but the main
target was to be wealthy quickly. That night an
indulgence in rose tinted beer glasses certainly affected
our rational thought process and fired our blurred
imagination and cognitive reasoning.

So one sunny morning, a few weeks after placing adverts in the local shops and conscripting my young family into posting hand produced leaflets through the unsuspecting letterboxes of what we deemed suitable or prospective clients across our neighbourhood, we began our adventure. With the old mower and tools secured in the trailer which was now bumping and swaying along behind my car, we set off. My new business partner sat sleepily beside me, dragging the very last whiff of smoke from a hand rolled cigarette now only a centimetre long as we headed for our very first client.

Eagerly we arrived at the location of our first destination; our customer was Mrs Wain, a small and pleasant lady of mature years who lived on a housing estate. Her front garden was small and consisted of a section of grass laughingly called a lawn, with one tired looking flower bed running along one side. I say flower bed in the broadest possible term, no flowers grew apart from weeds and three limp and stunted shrubs stood like dejected sentinels of a time when the garden had been resplendent in colour long ago. The back garden could almost be described as large compared to those pocket handkerchief gardens found on more modern housing estates, but it was still only twice the size of the front and I had estimated it would only take an hour to cut the grass front and back and pull a few weeds. I was mistaken! As I have already stated, my knowledge of horticulture could have been written on the back of a daisy leaf with room to spare. I had no real conception about the art of weeding, in truth I had little idea what a weed actually was; hence I assumed removing weeds would be a simple matter and over in moments. I repeat I was not experienced in the back breaking chore of horticulture. Nor did I realise that machinery of any description could be as temperamental as a spoilt child.

While waiting for responses to our adverts, we had repeatedly checked, rechecked and serviced the old mower in preparation for the expected onslaught of work and profit that would eventually turn both of us into prosperous businessmen. We both hoped that as gardeners, we would soon be raking it in but it soon became apparent it was no bed of roses. Humping the machine from the trailer along with a hand full of tools, we set about portraying the impression we actually knew what we were doing. Positioning the mower on the slightly sloping lawn, I checked the fuel, turned the throttle lever to the run setting, grasped the pull start handle and pulled. Nothing! Okay I thought; this is not unusual for a Briggs and Stratton petrol engine to require a number of pulls to gain ignition. I pulled the start cord again, and again, and again and several more times before releasing the handle which whipped back into the spring coil with a snap. Wiping the sweat from my brow I examined the offending machine with a growing sense of hate. Why had the damn thing decided to play up at the start of our very first job?

Sensing my desire to throw the thing from a great height or rearrange its appearance with a large hammer, my business partner strolled over and began examining the mower with an air of confidence. A confidence born from a total ignorance of the stubborn mechanical demon that sat smugly on the front lawn. This examination was swiftly followed by him clutching the starting handle that was attached to a string which in turn was attached to the spring coil upon the mower. I watched with a grin, quietly hoping the malicious machine would tear his arm off, not out of spite – well yes I suppose it was with spite as I was no longer in the eager and cheerful mood in which I began the day. With a loud grunt he gave a mighty pull, bending his back and whipping back his arm as he attempted to spring the inert machine into life. Predictably it did not happen, instead the result was a choking sound and red face as my partner coughed and sputtered out the cigarette butt he had almost swallowed in his efforts. The mower itself showed no signs of life or consideration and remained inert in the morning sunshine. My partner however required a few moments of gasping great lung fills of air and hands resting on knees following this single exertion.

Finally regaining his health and sanity he attacked the green mechanical monster once again with a whispered curse and gave it a kick which bothered the mower not one jot, my partner in response began hopping on one foot as pain shot through his toes as a result of the over enthusiastic kick. When the ritual dance was completed, he once more grasped the handle and gave another huge tug, and then another, and another and several more until finally collapsing upon the grass in a sweaty quivering heap of dejection and defeat. Not one puff of smoke, no spark of possible life nor any other sign came from the machine to give a hint that it may start despite all his efforts. If a machine could laugh, I swear that evil mower would be in hysterics.

'Well that's sodded that!' he gasped, 'we can't start the damn thing so how are we going to cut the damn grass?'

'Is there a problem young man?' came a quiet voice from a window behind us.

Mrs Wain had been watching our antics from her kitchen window and now concern showed on her face as she stared at my prostrate partner. Mrs Wain was a small lady in her late sixties, possibly seventies or even eighties, I was unsure so it may be best to simply describe her as of mature years. Her grey hair still showed evidence of the dark hues of younger days and black rimmed glasses perched upon her nose giving a librarian appearance to her lined face. A gold coloured chain flowed down from the side arms of the spectacles and rested round her thin neck in readiness to hang the glasses when not in use. A thickly knitted cardigan topped a pleated skirt, thick wrinkled *Nora Batty* support tights and tartan fluffy slippers completed the vision.

'No problems Mrs Wain,' I answered, 'it seems our mower is refusing to work this morning but I'm sure we'll sort it soon.'

Mrs Wain smiled, 'I do have a small electric mower in my shed if yours will not start. You can use that if you wish, I don't mind what you use as long as the grass is cut. There are plenty of gardening tools in the shed as well.'

She was observing our rusty garden implements with some distain and a slightly raised eyebrow.

'Thank you. We'll give our machine one more try and if that doesn't work then we'll take up your offer and use your mower. Fear not, the grass will be cut today even if I have to use scissors!' I replied with a grin.

Suddenly my partner leaped to his feet faster than I had ever seen him move before. Both myself and Mrs Wain looked on in surprise as he quickly stepped towards the inanimate object sometimes described as a lawn mower. Muttering under his breath he reached down to the mower engine and to my utter disbelief and frustration, he swiftly reattached the lead to the spark plug. Following our last service of the machine, one of us had forgotten to replace the plug cap and lead to the spark plug. Strangely neither of us had noticed this important factor during our vicious battle to start the mower. Glaring at me with a silent accusation that it was my fault, he once again grasped the starting handle and with a quick pull the machine spluttered into life.

Within seconds the Suffolk Punch was running smoothly and my partner finally began the job of cutting the grass, though still muttering curses against my person in a voice too low to catch the ears of our customer. I considered pointing out the fact that he had also failed to notice that the spark plug was not connected but thought better of it. A Suffolk Punch haircut is not good for ones complexion.

'There we go, it won't take us long now. We'll have the grass cut in no time so what other jobs would you like us to do?' I asked while noting the time on my watch so I could present a bill that did not include the time spent fighting the now healthy green mechanical contraption.

In a quiet voice Mrs Wain gave me instructions on what she wanted before disappearing from the kitchen window, an obvious suggestion that I get on and do some work. Taking the hint I walked over to the offending area and sized up what actually needed doing. Of course I had no idea what was a weed and what was a plant worth keeping. Making sure Mrs Wain could not see me, I gestured to my horticultural experienced partner that I needed guidance. With no skill whatsoever he managed to manoeuvre the mower over to the part of the garden where I stood in total confusion. Without a word he pointed to the dandelions, plantains, groundsel and daisies that littered the selected flower bed. Off he motored behind the mower as I dropped to my knees and armed with a trowel, began to hoist the troublesome green matter from the soil. It was not long before I realised what happened to old gardeners when they retire. They slowly spade away and throw in the trowel.

Finally the hour was up and the front and rear grass was now trimmed nicely and the front flower bed was devoid of weeds. I felt some pride in the successful completion of an honest hours work, not counting of course the half hour spent trying to start our petrol mower. Mrs Wain appeared at her front window for a moment before moving to her back door as she studied the standard of our work and gently nodded her approval. With an offer of refreshments in the form of tea or coffee, she opened her purse and extracted the agreed remittance and placed it in my eagerly stretched out hand. Politely we refused her offer of refreshments, stating we had other jobs to attend and time was short. Of course we had no other jobs or clients on the immediate horizon but one does not proffer that information to a customer. With the cash snugly secured in my pocket, we began the task of loading the trailer and ensuring we left the property in a clean and tidy condition before leaving. Mrs Wain had requested that we return on a weekly basis in order to catch up on the other jobs she had in mind and to keep the grass under control. Happily we replied that we would and with a wave we left Mrs Wain to shuffle back into her home.

As we drove away I noticed several of her neighbours watching us leave, one was already entering Mrs Wain's garden but at that time I did not register the significance of these actions. In ignorance my only wish was that they did not intend calling the police and having us arrested for impersonating gardeners. The logistics of running a business was new to me and I failed to realise that word of mouth is still the very best form of advertising known to man, woman and beast. The fact that we had been watched and examined by other residents in the immediate area flew over my head on wings of ignorance. My brain kicked into gear sometime later, unfortunately quite a long time later, when I realised that those neighbours were inspecting our work and seeking Mrs Wain's opinion of us. If her replies were favourable then we could expect to receive more business, and in fact we did.

Over the next few weeks we managed to lure more customers and the business slowly began to grow. I purchased another petrol lawn mower of dubious age and ability, it was an old Hayter which had seen better days but it was cheap, it worked and it could cut almost anything. From boot sales, garages clear outs and flea markets we gradually replaced our rusty equipment with tools that still had some degree of original paint work on them. We even decided upon a name for our embryo business venture. We now called ourselves *Green Fingers* in an attempt to persuade potential customers that we were indeed horticultural experts. Proudly we adorned our new business name upon leaflets and business cards, obtained via a friendly local printer in exchange for a couple of hours tidying his garden. The printer was a friend of mine and had been in business for many years, I even had a part time job with him as a young boy, sweeping up all the waste paper and making endless cups of tea. Regrettably now he was quite an old man, but he was still very capable and still ran his small printing press regularly almost as a hobby.

Unfortunately these days he was often inclined to make the odd mistake or three. When I first approached him for the cards and leaflets, he was pleased to help and ran off a dozen card samples for me to check and use. Sadly I could not use those free samples at all. His age and deteriorating hearing had led to him producing a dozen cards announcing Green *Singers* gardening services. How I would define the purpose of such a service evaded me and still does. Gently I pointed out this minor, or possibly B flat mistake and he rectified it before printing out an amount of cards suitable to my limited financial resources. The mobile gardening and landscaping service of Green Fingers was now fully up and running.

Chapter Two: Winter work.

Business began to pick up slightly after some weeks of trying to survive on just a few customers and occasional odd jobs. Considering the fact that we had stupidly began our bright new venture in autumn, this came as no surprise. No intelligence there, any other fool would have waited until spring to initiate a gardening business but sadly, intelligence was not on our list of business acquisitions. Onwards we strove, fighting blisters, stings, cuts and other general abuse from Mother Nature and the horticultural environment. Our two mowers were still struggling on, though by now both were in the last epoch of life and we spent almost as much time fixing them as we did using them.

Winter was here and we were learning that people generally forgot their gardens during these cold months but there are always those exceptions, luckily. Our pitiful client list quickly shrunk again as September and October passed by and headed into November. Instead of gardening and earning money, I was forced to walk the streets posting leaflets through endless letterboxes in an attempt to promote our business. My erstwhile partner did not deem to accompany me on my lonely trek and I began to suspect his heart was not really in the business any more and the winter weather had dampened his spirits even more. So I slogged the icy streets, estates and business parks on my own, sometimes coercing my two young children to assist me with the promise of extra pocket money, but bribery soon lost its appeal and once again I trod the pavements alone.

Work was virtually non existent now so I subsidised my income by delivering sales catalogues along with my leaflets. Least I was getting paid while striving to become a successful businessman, and to avoid starving of course, and there were the bills lying forlornly upon the doormat to consider. Following the idea that money was good, especially with Christmas loaming, I took up part time work doing what ever I could to sustain my existence until spring could come to my rescue. However I did cling to the hope that one day my small business would thrive and so I continued to promote the firm of Green Fingers at every opportunity. My spirits were kept high by the number of enquiries I received from potential clients seeking to book our services once spring arrived, so I managed to persuade my family that I was not a failure yet, hopefully. I even attended a talk on gardening in the local village hall, the subject was *Bushes in the Garden* but I soon left; I could not get a word in hedge ways!

Some forward thinking people still considered their gardens even in mid winter and the occasional client still rang seeking our services. My partner however was growing more and more despondent with not only our lack of work, but also the utter distain he held for any form of manual labour. I never understood why a person with such a dislike for physical work would agree to being a partner in a gardening business. Let's face it; everyone understands that gardening is no bed of roses . . . Gardening is hard labour and there is no escaping the fact, cutting grass, digging and weeding flower and vegetable beds, pruning shrubs, trees and a whole range of unwanted garden guests such as the humble but well defended bramble. Another fact soon became apparent as we struggled on with our ancient lawn mowers; most gardens in Britain are not flat. A vast majority of the gardens in our area either slopped up hill or down hill, some even slid side ways and some were so steep they had to be tiered, and all had to be mown by sweating, panting and exhausted human wrecks, namely us. Luckily at this time of year the grass cutting duty was allowed to hibernate as frost or snow but mostly rain tempered the natural instincts of the

British horticultural hobbyist. Instead a profusion of bonfires, leaf clearing and pruning filled those cold bright sunny days that occasionally interspersed the typical English wet winter weather. Most of the small jobs we were called to undertake consisted of tidying wind and rain swept areas of desolation that in more pleasant climes were proudly identified as a garden.

Gardening in deep winter is a luxury most intelligent homeowners strongly avoid, and in truth the normal domestic landscape requires little attention as nature slumbers through the bleakest months. But as with all interests, hobbies or pleasures, there are exceptions, those brave or mentally challenged persons who continue to heap care and attention on their would be castle grounds with no respect for the time of year or the howling weather conditions. It was not long before we received a phone call from such a person.

White glittering frost lay like Gary Glitter's bed sheet over the ground and a freezing wind chapped the faces and hands of those struggling on journeys to work, school or the shops. A bright blue crystal clear sky illuminated by a weak winter sun canopied the frozen land early that morning when my phone rang. Expecting only one of those annoying call centres trying to sell me something I did not want. Or to inform me my computer had a fault that only they could fix, providing I sent a large cheque to some unidentifiable location in India. However I was surprised when a voice enquired if this was the number for Green Fingers. Quickly I gathered my wits and replied that it was and to whom was I speaking. The caller was a Mrs Pollard-Brown and she was in desperate need of a person to attend her garden. I then routinely enquired when she wanted the work to be undertaken and was again surprised when she requested our help as soon as possible, in fact that very day if feasible. Mrs Pollard-Brown explained that her husband was a local vicar and did not have the time to spend gardening, so the bulk of the work was left to her. Of course I made some feeble pretence of checking my work diary before replying that we did in fact have a vacant space in our busy day and we could be at her property within the hour. With a relieved tone Mrs Pollard-Brown gave me her address and stated she would await our arrival.

With my mind in turmoil I immediately phoned my partner and informed him we had a job to attend. His response was none too polite but eventually he agreed to leave his warm bed and be ready when I called to pick him up in thirty minutes. I said thirty minutes because I knew he would still be drinking tea and dragging on cigarettes when I arrived, so by stating thirty minutes I may be able to prise him from his home in about fifty minutes, giving us plenty of time to reach our destination inside an hour. With a brief explanation to my wife, I charged from my house to begin loading my car and trailer with equipment. Having no idea what work Mrs Pollard-Brown wanted, I decided to load both mowers and all our tools just in case. Humping the mowers into the trailer brought several amazed and bemused stares from my neighbours as the idea of cutting frost covered grass cast doubt on my sanity. Nevertheless ensuring I had included every ground working tool I owned was a decision that was to prove fortunate.

After satisfying myself that every possible piece of equipment was loaded to cover every eventuality I soon realised how cold the day was. Rubbing my hands in a vain effort to warm them up, I ran back inside and sought out some suitable working clothes. Thermal underwear, thick jeans, several jumpers, two pairs of socks and a padded jacket encased my body in the hope of staying warm for more than just a few seconds. A woolly hat pulled tightly down over my ears while a pair of thermal gloves provided some insulation under my stronger working gloves. I was ready. I knew I would be freezing before long but I had done my best to prepare myself and now I resembled a large fabric ball as I waddled out to my car and trailer. Finally with a cheerful wave goodbye to my family I set off to rouse my unwilling partner and face what ever challenge awaited us at the residence of Mrs Pollard-Brown.

As expected it took me some time to galvanise my still sleepy partner into a resemblance of action and once both secure in the car, we headed of to our intended destination. My business partner was older than me, marching into his fortieth decade, medium height and build. Dark hair was rapidly vacating his scalp leaving patches of pale skin bare to the elements. A square face, brown hound dog eyes and a short beard protruded from a thick scarf as he sat slumped in the front passenger seat of my vehicle. On the short journey I began to realise just how much my partner disliked our choice of employment. For most of his life he had worked in factories and other establishments that offered protection from the elements raging outside. Being dragged from his bed and forced out into a freezing morning did little to improve his mood as he fogged out my car with his incessant chain smoking. However at that point I did not comprehend just how his feelings of resentment against undertaking physical

labour in the out door environment dismayed him. I was
to find out later.

Without mishap we eventually arrived at the
abode of Mrs Pollard-Brown. Silently we viewed her
home and garden before venturing out from the warm
car. The property was in one of the more affluent areas
and the garden was quite large but thankfully flat, a fact
we both recognised with relief. Lawns, flower beds,
rose beds and shrubs were surrounded by a hedge of
assorted bushes and small trees on three sides, while a
low plant crowned wall secured both sides of the path to
her front door. From what we could see through the
misted car windows, a green house and vegetable or
fruit plot lay to the rear of her bungalow but more than
that we could not ascertain from our position beside the
curb that ran along parallel to the front of her property.

After surveying the property for several
moments, we reluctantly exited the warm car and braced
ourselves against the cold. Walking up to her door I
rang the bell and stood shivering as I waited her
appearance. Almost immediately the door was opened
to reveal a tall but thin grey haired woman in her
seventies I guessed. Dressed in a thick tweed skirt,
frilly collared blouse and a long woollen cardigan, she

peered down at me as if I was a brush salesman trying
his luck.

'Good morning,' I greeted, 'Green Fingers
gardening services.'

'Oh. Good morning. Thank you for arriving so
promptly. Please wait while I get my coat and I'll show
you what I want done. Are you on your own?'

'No ma'am, my colleague is with me,' I replied
while indicating a miserable shivering wreck still
standing beside my car. I noticed he had adorned his
balding palate with an old cloth cap while the remnants
of yet another hand rolled cigarette stump hung limply
and cold from his tightly clenched lips.

'Good. One person would take too long and I
want the beds tidied before my visitors arrive for lunch.
I simply cannot stand an untidy garden,' replied Mrs
Pollard-Brown as she reached for a coat hanging on the
wall beside the door and swiftly wrapped herself in it.

Quickly glancing round at the immaculate
landscape in wonderment I made the mistake of opening
my mouth. 'It's a lovely garden and I cannot see there is
much to do really,' I said.

'Oh there's a huge amount to do! Just because
it's a little chilly does not mean my garden should look
a mess. The flower beds need weeding and fluffing, the

lawn edges need trimming, and while I do understand
that it's no use cutting the lawns but at least the edges
can be tidy. Then there's simply mountain's of pruning
to do, leaves to clear and manure to dig in before
spring,' listed Mrs Pollard-Brown with the dignity of
royalty.

'Certainly ma'am, we'll get right to it. Now if
you could point out which area you wish us to begin?' I
replied suitably chastised while still pondering the
practice of *fluffing* flower beds.

Walking with great care on this cold morning,
Mrs Pollard-Brown led me off to one side of her
bungalow while I gestured for my partner to join us.
Halting in front of a large flower bed approximately six
foot wide and fifteen foot long Mrs Pollard-Brown
pointed at some very small weeds with a tut.

'This bed is a disgrace! It needs to be weeded
and fluffed up so it is tidy for when my guests arrive.
Please do not simply pull the weeds out; I want them
dug out, including the roots so they will not reappear
within a few days. Can you do that?' she asked in a
rather stern voice.

With growing despair I stared down at the
offending bed, covered with frost and obviously frozen
solid. I knew this would be horrendous, trying to dig

into and remove small weeds from ground that resembled concrete rather than soil. I glanced across at my partner, hoping he may put forward a comment on the condition of the soil so I could possibly reinforce the comments with my own and endeavour to utter the perfect excuse that would allow us to escape from the almost impossible task she had set before us. But alas, with a cold pinched gloomy expression, my partner just shrugged his shoulders and left me to it. Under my breath I made rude comments about his parentage, accused him of possible bestiality and certain lack of intelligence.

'No problems ma'am, we'll soon have this bed looking spic and span,' I answered with the biggest and most confident smile I could muster, 'it shouldn't take long so we'll get started right away.'

'Thank you young man, please let me know when you have finished and I'll come and check.' With that off she shuffled into the house.

'Why didn't you say something?' I demanded of my partner as he strode slowly across the lawn towards me and then glared down at the offending flower bed with its blanket of frost and ice. Reaching the edge of the bed, he shoved his hands deep into his pockets with his head bowed over the area on which we were to work. A deep sigh escaped his lips and for one moment I thought he was going to burst into tears!

'I thought I'd let you be boss,' he eventually replied, 'I don't really like talking to people. So how are we going to do this then?'

'Well I suppose we'd best get some trowels, a bucket and something to kneel on. I think this is going to be difficult.'

'It's going to be bloody cold!' he stated unnecessarily as we headed to the car to collect our tools.

Finally with tools at hand, kneeling mats in place and hands suitably gloved, we both eyed the ground before us with trepidation. I could see several small plants lying stiff in the cold soil, but as my gardening knowledge was limited to say the least, I checked with my partner what plants to keep and which were weeds to remove. With a finger that was rapidly turning blue, he pointed out the Hairy Bittercress, Groundsel, Daisies, Plantains and Dandelions to be removed. Of course I recognised the Dandelions because I had rabbits and guinea pigs as a child; however all the other stuff was just so much greenery left over from warmer times, pre ice age.

When my partner was satisfied I was not going to pull out anything of interest we began. With unrehearsed synchronization we both stabbed our trowels at the cold earth, and jarred our arms right up to the shoulder, recalling in pain and surprise. The ground was so frozen and hard, our hand tools would not penetrate it, and in fact they did not even disturb the surface at all.

'Well that's a bugger!' muttered my partner, 'now how are we going to manage?'

Rubbing my sore hand I glared at the vicious and nasty ground while wishing I had a bazooka; that would sort out those damn weeds! Still using some choice words in between shivers, I set off back to the trailer to collect a fork and spade.

'Let's try something a bit heavier, which one do you want, forking thing or the spade?' I asked.

'I'll take that forking thing,' he replied while reaching out to grasp the implement, 'it's a bit like taking a sledge hammer to a nail, but I'll give it a go.'

With that said he whipped up the fork and shot it down towards the earth. At an even greater velocity the fork bounced right back and almost threw him backwards as the ground once more thwarted his efforts. With the fork prongs ringing in perfect pitch but

completely out of tune with the stream of words
emitting from his clenched teeth, my partner dropped
the offending forking thing onto the lawn in disgust. It
took some effort on my part to avoid giving freedom to
the mirth that threatened to burst forth as I watch him
stomping around with his hands shoved tightly between
his legs in an attempt to ease the sting that resulted from
hitting a solid surface with the fork. I had the uncanny
notion that if I erupted in laughter at that point, I may
find that innocent looking fork being aimed at one of
my more tender body parts.

'It's no damn use!' he shouted upon completion
of his amusing jig across the frosty lawn, 'if the ground
is too hard for a fork, what the hell are we going to do?'

Scratching my head I replied with a hint of
dejection, 'There's one thing left but I have no idea if
it'll work. Let's try the pick axe, if that doesn't work
we'll have to tell Mrs Pollard-Brown that she'll have to
wait for a warmer day when her ground defrosts.'

I retrieved the pick axe from the trailer, silently
thankful that I had decided to load every tool we
possessed. However the task was still not completed and
the ground not penetrated so maybe I was counting my
chickens too early. Walking back over to the flower
bed, I positioned myself with the pick axe held firmly in

my freezing hands. With all the force I could muster I swung the pick axe down towards the ground and those hideous specks of green called weeds that were held in such revulsion by our client. Down swept the pick head, down through the frost blanket and down into the frozen ground, driving deep into the soil. I shouted with glee and my partner smiled in what I assumed to be satisfaction, however our joy was short lived. Still smiling I pulled at the pick handle to remove it from the ground, and it did not move. It was now stuck fast and deep in the cold soil.

To my added horror, Mrs Pollard-Brown chose that moment to come out and inspect our work. On silent slippers she stalked up behind us as we both now struggled to tear the pick axe from the ground. It was fortunate that the exertion involved in the extraction of the tool took all our breath, not realising she was now behind us, our language would have no doubt been a tad more colourful than is perhaps appropriate for the ears of a lady of mature years.

'And how are we doing?' came a quiet question. It was a question that initiated an immediate response in action rather than in words. Both my partner and I had been so engrossed in removing the stuck fast pick axe that a voice suddenly sounding behind us resulted in our feet leaving the ground as we leapt up in surprise.

'I'm sorry,' said Mrs Pollard-Brown, 'did I startle you?'

'Er, just slightly,' I replied as I waited for my heart rate to fall back to its normal level.

'Oh I am sorry. Anyway I thought I would see how you're getting on. You've been here a while now but I can see you've been having some difficulty. Is the ground hard?'

'Yes it most definitely is frozen solid I'm afraid. We have tried several tools but I think it's going to be just too hard to dig this morning. I'm sorry but nature has beaten us today,' I stated in response while readying myself for her accusations of failure.

'I understand,' she said, 'but it doesn't matter because my visitors have cancelled for today and there is now no rush to tidy the garden. However I wonder if you could do one or two other tasks for me instead?'

'Certainly. If we can. What would you like us to do for you?'

'Well those trees are beginning to obstruct my view, could you remove a few of the lower branches d'you think?'

Before answering I turned to examine the said trees, but to my consternation my partner decided it was time he actually said something and agreed we would prune the trees for her. With a smile Mrs Pollard-Brown shuffled back across the lawn and disappeared back into the warmth of her home.

Angrily I spun round to confront my partner. 'Why did you agree to that?' I demanded.

'Well she only wants a few branches cut off. I think we should be able to handle that.'

'Have you looked at the trees in question?' I asked him.

'No I haven't but how hard can it be?'

'Take a look now,' I suggested and so he turned round and for the first time, took a close examination of the task he had accepted.

'Oh crap!'

'Yep! Not so easy to just prune a few branches is it?' I growled.

The trees in question were tall Leylandii that had already had their lower branches removed, leaving approximately nine foot of clear space between the first boughs and the ground. On a cold, frosty and very slippery morning, my partner had agreed to a task we were even less prepared for than excavating frozen solid soil! We had no ladder or chainsaw and neither of us had any liking for heights, so achieving this new task could be interesting. Silently we both stared in apprehension at the towering trees that lined one side of the property. I cannot speak for my partner's thoughts at this stage, but I will admit my first thought was to flee the scene at a rapid run.

The sensation of panic subsided and I suggested we investigate the possibility that Mrs Pollard-Brown might have a ladder situated upon her property so we set off in search. Within moments we had discovered a ladder hanging on brackets attached to a small shed at the rear of the property. Lifting the ladder between us, we retraced our steps back to the leylandii hedge which was fast taking on the appearance of a monstrous forest. Carefully we positioned the ladder up against the first tree near one of the lowest limbs. I could see what Mrs Pollard-Brown meant when she had said the branches still obscured her view. Not more than half a mile behind her leylandii barrier was a perfect view of the glittering sea and coast line. The removal of just a few more branches would enable her to easily enjoy this view from her lounge window.

With the ladder lying against the trunk I retrieved the piece of rope I used to secure the mowers in the trailer and climbed the ladder while my partner hung onto its base. I tied the top rung of the ladder to a nearby branch, making sure it was not one of those to be removed, with me still on it. When safely attached and firm, I then tackled the question; did I include a saw when I loaded the trailer this morning? Climbing carefully down from that staggering height, I requested my partner check for a saw in amongst the tools. In moments he had found one and strode back to hand it to me.

'Here hang on,' I said, 'this was your bright idea so you can cut the first branch.'

My partner recoiled in fright, 'I can't go up there.'

'So why the hell did you agree to it?'

'Well I didn't want to say no, especially seeing as we couldn't do the weeding.'

'Surprisingly it's easier to say *No* than falling from a tree,' I retorted.

'Ok, ok I'll have a go, but you make sure you hold onto that ladder properly. If I fall I'll make sure I land on you.'

'Go for it!' I said as he took his first tentative step upon the ladder.

Up the ladder he went, legs quivering and saw clasped tightly in one gloved hand while the other gripped the ladder rungs as if his life depended on it. A light almost imperceptible breeze fluttered by the ladder which caused my partner to lunge forward closer to the ladder and hold on with all available limbs and any other part of his anatomy that was humanly possible. He was only on the second rung!

'Keep the damn thing steady!' he whispered, 'I hate heights and this ladder doesn't feel safe at all. Can't we do this another time?'

I looked on in pity, and some malevolence. Should I offer to climb the ladder myself? Or stand back and watch the shaking wreck struggle a while longer? I decided to wait for a few more minutes, if only to see if he could actually make the third rung. Finally I relented, the third rung was obviously an insurmountable task and we were running out of time.

'Okay, down you come. I'll cut the branch and you can do the next one. Pass down the saw first; I don't really want to become a split personality.'

Gratefully he complied, handing me down the saw before slowly, very slowly climbing off the second rung of the ladder. Once he was safely down on terra firma, I took my place upon the ladder and swiftly climbed up to within reach of the targeted branch. I had little love for heights either but nine or ten foot up on a ladder firmly roped to a tree on a calm sunny day was not quite enough to send me into hysteria. Grasping the saw in one hand I began the slow and strenuous business of cutting through four inches of wet and cold wood. Obviously the saw had seen better days and certainly sharper days so the progress of amputation took its time. Finally with a loud snap the branch parted from the tree and fell to the ground, missing my partner by inches as he was busy rolling another cigarette. A sight that amused me greatly, especially as it was his fault I was up a tree in freezing winter weather. With a sigh, I shuffled my position slightly to enable me to reach the second of several branches that had to be removed in order to improve Mrs Pollard-Brown's view of the sea.

Some two hours later the job was completed and a stack of dismembered tree limbs lay in an untidy pile on the edge of the lawn. I was drenched in sweat and had long ago stripped down to my first layer of wool while my partner stood shivering with cold. Obviously I had been lumbered with the entire task of climbing the ladder and sawing off branches so I had become very warm, contrary to my partner who had only the minor effort of holding the ladder for the last two hours. I will admit I was not overflowing with sympathy for his plight at this point. Silence descended, ending the sounds of the saw rasping through unyielding wood, the grunts, groans and occasion choice word from my self and the stifled yawns from my partner. Again Mrs Pollard-Brown reappeared like an apparition beside us. Quietly she surveyed the work done, or wanton destruction of trees, which ever way one views it.

'That's better. My view of the water is now improved; I really enjoy the sight of the sea, especially in the stormy weather. Now, when are you going to remove all these branches from my lawn? I cannot possibly have them lying there making my garden untidy so they must be removed immediately,' announced Mrs Pollard-Brown with a tone of distain in her already haughty voice.

'Pardon me? Do you mean we have to take all these branches away?' I asked in a shocked voice. The removal of the amputated branches had not occurred to me, I had assumed we would simply stack them away in some secluded spot at the rear of her property.

'Of course I want you to take them away, I have no room nor any wish for them to remain in my garden. My husband simply does not have the time and we are both getting on in years, so I will require you to remove them. I will of course pay you the extra for your time and the removal of these branches.'

Mrs Pollard-Brown replied in a voice almost as shocked as mine. It was obvious the thought of us not removing the branches had not occurred to her either.

The mention of more money immediately swept aside my shock and replaced it with greed. Unconsciously I rubbed my hands together as I replied that we would happily remove said branches and would amend the bill accordingly. At that moment however, I had absolutely no idea what I was going to do with a heap of leylandii branches so I decided to load them into the trailer and see what opportunities arose later. Swiftly we began loading up, piling branches on top of the two un-needed mowers and scrabbling round to find more rope or even string with which to tie the load down. Successful at last with the load secured and my partner out of harms way and sat in my car; I approached the front door in readiness to receive our just rewards. Suddenly I stopped. I had no idea what to charge for the disposal of the leylandii or how long the task would take. Pondering this problem for a moment I decided to simply count it as an extra hours labour and arrived at a price. Happy now, I rang the door bell and awaited Mrs

Pollard-Brown. After some pleasantries and the receipt of cash, we were on our way home. Mrs Pollard-Brown had praised our work and booked us on a weekly basis for the foreseeable future. Now all we had to do was dispose of the trailer full of branches, a task I was still uncertain how to accomplish. I decided to take my partner back to his home and then proceed to my own home and contemplate the problem after a warming cup of tea.

Arriving home I entered and handed over the cash to my wife as she understands money much better than I do, and the fact that I would get no cup of tea nor a meal or any form of refreshment until I did so. I had already paid my partner his share of the day's earnings so what was left was – hers. Gratefully I sipped at a steaming cup of tea before mentioning to my wife about the problem of the branches. Saying nothing she stared at me for a moment before indicating the warmth giving Rayburn beside me, a Rayburn that could burn anything and, yep, wood was ideal. So to finish the day of sawing down tree limbs in the freezing cold, I had to carry the branches to my back garden and once more set about the task of sawing. I had to cut up all the branches into log sized shapes that could be burnt in our solid fuel burner. By the end of the day my right arm was hanging limp and I threw the saw into my shed with the fervent hope of never seeing it again!

Chapter Three: And then Bob came along.

Following the fiasco at the property of Mrs Pollard-
Brown, my reluctant business partner decided he had
had enough and wanted to leave the business. He stated
he did not want to work as a gardener anymore as he
found the work too demanding and uncomfortable, plus
he was fed up with being cold and wet and being out in
all weathers. I did question his sanity with his next piece
of news, he told me he had landed a job as a postman
and was due to start the following week. Okay I
thought, he does not like being out in all weather
conditions, he is fed up with being cold and wet, so he
gets a job as a postman. Some how his logic escaped me
but I wished him the best anyway.

I did not really mind being left as the sole
proprietor of Green Fingers as there was not yet enough
work for two and I could carry on by myself for a while.
Our parting was very amicable as we were friends
before and remain friends to this day. We decided to
split the tools and equipment between us, but as it
turned out, my now ex-business partner only wanted the
old Suffolk Punch lawn mower. To be honest I was
delighted to see the damn thing go, it had caused no end
of problems with its temperamental attitude and

inability to actually work for a whole day. I know that machine was not a living entity but I swear that thing was possessed all the same. As soon as we needed it in earnest it would refuse to start, and it had a knack of breaking down halfway through cutting a lawn. I still think it did these things deliberately. With a handshake we parted and I was left with the old Hayter mower and most of the tools along with the trailer which was mine anyway.

I returned home to inform my family of the news and was met with a thunderous roar of indifference at my proclamation. With head bowed I began sorting out what equipment I had that could still realistically bear the title of a gardening tool, and decided I desperately needed to update and increase my tiny store of tools. With a pitiful expression and eyes as sad as I could possibly portray, I approached my boss, namely the wife and asked if I could purchase a new lawn mower as I could not continue with just the Hayter. To my utter surprise she agreed so off we both set to try our luck with the local bank manager. He too agreed after hearing my hastily constructed business plan and examining my short list of existing clients, and allowed us a small loan. Still in the thrones of success we left the bank and headed of in search of a brand new lawn mower.

For the next couple of weeks I managed to run the business on my own with a reasonable amount of success, which basically means I did not get sued by anyone nor did I injure myself or any other person, animal or loitering television gardening personality. Slowly the business grew as winter turned into spring and people suddenly remembered that the area of waste land outside their back door was in fact a garden. My new mower began to earn its living and I grew muscles on calluses as I pushed, pulled and dragged the shining red machine over countless acres of lawns. Clients began ringing at all times of the day, and sometimes even night, requesting my services and the list of customers increased almost daily. I had increased my charges as after some in depth paperwork and accounting, I had realised I would not survive on what I was charging. Even this did not deter the growth of Green Fingers and finally I decided I needed help.

I could not offer full time employment, nor could I guarantee a full week's work as obviously the characteristics of the British weather made planning a work list virtually impossible. Bearing in mind the uncertainty of the work, the hours offered and the weather, I decided to search for an employee by word of mouth. I began asking all my friends and family if anyone wanted a few days work each week over the summer months. The responses were immediately negative and those even remotely repeatable were discounted along with the more unmentionable ones. Still I persevered and eventually was informed about a character who was actively searching for work, a rarity in the local area. Discovering where this individual could be found, I made my way to that destination with a despondent attitude, I had begun to lose faith in the idea of having someone help me on such an irregular employment basis.

Upon arrival at the address given, I knocked on the door and asked if the he was available. Without receiving an answer I was invited into the house by a burly chap and was slightly disturbed when several of the individuals already in the room began to slowly edge towards the door. There are about half a dozen persons in the small lounge like room, some I will admit appeared slightly shifty. I wondered if I had unwittingly stumbled into the hideout of the local village mafia and pondered if I would soon be wearing concrete welly boots. The burly gentleman who appeared to be the spokesman, or chief assassin, I could not quite make up my mind as to which, questioned why I wanted to speak to that person, and it was only when I informed them who I was that they finally relented and called out for him to attend. The thudding of footsteps upon a staircase foretold my new employee's eminent arrival and I found myself eagerly awaiting my first sight of this person who was guarded so faithfully by those who shared his residence. Suddenly there he stood, a stocky man standing about five foot six inches tall with fair but receding hair and lopsided glasses perched on his nose. Eyeing me suspiciously he held out his hand and introductions were made. My prospective new employee was called Bob, least that's what he insisted on being called, and as it was a simple name to remember I was happy to go alone with his wish. Discovering my reasons for calling, his face lit up in a huge grin and the atmosphere lightened immediately. I decided I liked this character and took up his offer of refreshments as we sat and discussed the possible employment opportunities. I explained as fully as I could what would be expected of him and asked if he had any experience or knowledge of horticulture and gardening. He stated that he had a good knowledge and some experience. I was soon to learn that this was not in fact the case but no harm was done as I had no idea either. Finally we agreed that he would work for me on a self employed basis and we settled on a date and time for him to start.

The others in the room had been trying hard to pretend they were not listening or interested in our conversation, however when the agreement was reached, broad smiles broke out like a gathering of Lewis Carroll's Cheshire cat impersonators. Tea and coffee began to flow freely and I suddenly found myself faced with a mountain of questions about Green Fingers and the type of work I undertook. At first I was very cagey in my responses, however it did not take me long to figure out that no one in the room was even remotely interested in stealing my business ideas. In fact the very idea of physical labour appalled the majority of them while the mere mention of work sent the others in to spasms of shock. Finally about an hour after I had arrived, I managed to escape the genial gathering and make my way home.

The first day with Bob turned out to be quite uneventful. I ensured we tackled only the easiest of jobs that day so I could ascertain exactly what he was capable of. I soon learnt that he was a willing worker and would undertake any job with a smile and plenty of effort. Sometimes there was more effort than necessary but at least the task was completed. It soon became apparent that Bob was a very genial character and we spent much of the day in good humour with frequent laughter, it was obvious we were going to get along fine.

There was one drawback which came to light very soon as we began our working relationship, neither of us had any idea about horticulture. I had learnt about some plant and weed identification from my ex-business partner but it was evident that Bob had little or no knowledge of anything that was green and had leaves. This should have been a disaster but instead it became an advantage. Once again at Mrs Wain's property, we had been instructed to cut back the foliage of perennial shrubs that lined a border beside the path that lead to the rear of the garden. Both Bob and I viewed the contents of the chosen bed in confusion and uncertainty. What were we supposed to cut, how were we supposed to cut it and how much should we cut off? Grasping a pair of shears in my hand I studied a large plant which had stems cascading down over the small wall that separated the path from the bed. I scratched my head then yelled in surprise, I had unthinkingly used the hand which held the shears. Luckily the shears were closed so all I received was a thump on the head and a few stars succeeded by one or two appropriate words before deciding not to do that again.

When my vision cleared I returned to staring at the plant in question and seeing my indecision, Bob came over to offer his advice and like a fool I listened. Bob knowingly identified the plant as a stinging nettle and suggested I cut it back to the ground before attempting to dig it out in its entirety. As the plant did resemble a stinging nettle I agreed with his suggestion and set about hacking the thing to pieces.

'Don't trim that one back too much please,' called Mrs Wain's voice from her kitchen window, 'it'll flower soon and I love to see it in full bloom.'

My hands froze immediately and my brain went into overdrive. 'No problem Mrs Wain,' I said with as much confidence as I could muster, 'I'm only giving it a tidy so it does not obstruct the path too much.'

'That's fine however I think you should start on that hydrangea over there.'

I was delighted to see she was actually pointing at the shrub in question. 'Just prune it down to the last double bud on each branch so I will still get plenty of flowers later.'

I agreed and after clearing the stems from the unidentified plant, I moved on to attack the hydrangea with gratitude. I was convinced Mrs Wain had realised she had Messrs Dumb and Dumber working in her garden and had discreetly decided to education us. From her window she then instructed Bob to begin working on clearing the winter debris that littered the small raised flower bed located immediately outside her back door. Mrs Wain instructed Bob that all he should remove was those dead stems, leaves and other such detritus but leave anything that was still green and not a weed. Bob happily consented and knelt down over the edge of the bed to begin his work. When Mrs Wain had withdrawn from the window, I hastened over to Bob and quickly pointed out what was a weed and what was not before returning to the hydrangea with gusto.

The hydrangea was large so it took me most of our allotted time to prune the branches and clear up the waste. I stuffed everything into numerous black bin bags before moving on to assist Bob in his own clear up. Finally we were finished and knocked at her back door to receive payment. I must admit I was apprehensive as I was sure she would cancel any future work and send us on our way as incompetent numbskulls in the practice of gardening. To my surprise Mrs Wain

appeared delighted with the work we had done and paid
me without hesitation. Then while Bob went off to store
the tools and load the black bags into the trailer, Mrs
Wain peered at me closely before dropping her voice
and making a suggestion that I was delighted to hear.

'I don't think you know much about gardening
do you?' she questioned first.

I replied that in truth we did not but were trying
to learn and would work hard at whatever task we were
given. She seemed satisfied with this reply and stated
that she would guide us in future and that we could seek
her knowledge in any aspect of horticulture. She added
that as she was now virtually housebound due to a
disability, helping to teach us would be a pleasure. Well
I could have kissed her for her kindness but I refrained,
partly due to it being inappropriate and partly due to the
fact her moustache was far better than mine!

For a few weeks all went well in our little world
of gardening, grass cutting and other assorted tasks
relating to horticulture. The name of Green Fingers was
slowly getting around the neighbourhood and business
was flourishing. The use of my car with a trailer was
now insufficient for our needs so I bit the bullet and
bought an old transit van which then doubled as a
family car and a works van, much to the dubious delight

of my family. Shopping trips and days out in a van with only three seats between four family members lead to some slight disagreements on a regular basis, though I was alright as I was the driver and my seat was secure. Finally I was forced to fit extra seats and seat belts in the back and insert a window into the sliding side door. I might add that the vehicle seating and seat belt laws were not so stringent at that time and I managed to get away with perhaps more liberties than I would in these modern times.

The van did provide much entertainment when the family went off on a day trip. All the equipment was cleared from the back of the van and blankets and cushions were spread over the floor and made an acceptable playing area for the kids, this in turn helped avoid those stressful moments in any journey by forestalling that dreaded and constantly repeated question that plagues all parents:

'Are we there yet?'

The business had not yet filled the diary to an extent where I could not take the occasional extra day off during the kids' holidays, in fact there were still too many days when no work was booked and the phone did not ring. In the main however, business was increasing at a steady rate and we began to add business premises to our client lists. The list of private clientele was increasing mainly by word of mouth, for example Mrs X told Mrs Y that we were good workers and did not overly charge for our work. Often almost a whole estate would require our services and we would simply walk from one client to another, one garden to another. Obviously this was an ideal situation for me as it greatly reduced the time and cost of travelling between jobs, however it was very hard word as there were few chances of a break or rest as we rushed from garden to garden like grass splattered garden gnomes making a vain attempt at freedom.

One business that requested our services was a medium sized campsite that catered for those who wished to experience life under canvass or in a caravan or preferred the luxury of a small chalet. The main area consisted of static caravans surrounded by huge prairies of grass which the campsite proprietor required us to maintain to a suitable height that small children and dogs could be clearly seen, but the by products of both children and animals remained hidden from sight. This of course created a very aesthetic scene, until one stepped in a pile of dog poo that lay in ambush for the unwary camper, or was run over by a lawn mower which had the effect of splattering the offending mess over a wider area, and of course the poor grass cutter.

Situated at one end of the site were the dozen or so chalets, all with small lawns in front of the buildings and even smaller patches of grass at the rear. At the other end of the campsite was an area set aside for tents of all shapes and sizes, from the one man tent favoured by those strange solo hikers to the bungalow sized tents that offered shelter to families accompanied by hordes of screaming, hyperactive and unruly children - and a dog, naturally!

Upon receiving the contact to maintain this campsite over the holiday months, I had once again invested in a new mower, a larger one this time that would enable us to mow the site in the shortest possible time. It was very hard work as the site was situated on a slight slope and we constantly had to avoid running children and dogs and drunken adults who wandered purposefully in front of our mowers with a supercilious attitude brought on by the fact that they were on holiday and we were not. This superior assumption annoyed me immensely and I soon discovered a form of entertainment that left me feeling content. With a smile I would enquire if these arrogant campers were enjoying their holidays amidst the typical wet British weather.

They would all state with a forced smile that they were indeed enjoying their chosen holiday venue before enquiring if I also took my vacations in a similar setting. In the best offhand manner I could muster, I would reply that I would not even consider such a place for my holiday, and as the summer was my busiest period, I did not take a break during this season. Instead I would explain that I holidayed in the Algarve or the Canary Islands during the winter months. Of course this was a blatant lie but they did not know this and I was rewarded by the looks of astonishment and envy that replaced the arrogant expressions upon their faces. With a polite but shocked comment on how delightful those destinations were, the now downcast camper would wander off and strive to avoid us for the remainder of their stay in the wet, cold and typically over expensive accommodation provided by the majority of British camp sites.

The vast majority of all those camping were not obnoxious to us as we struggled to cut the grass areas within the time allowed by our contract. Many of the campers we met over the years we spent maintaining that camp site were every pleasant and friendly, not all those staying there were surrounded by noisy children or barking, crapping dogs. There were many older couples seeking fresh air and peace in a rural location close to the sea, younger couples also frequented the site in an attempt to ensure seclusion for their emotions to bloom and their intimacy to remain anonymous. Couples with older teenage children and groups of friends, visitors from other countries and the occasional celebrity in disguise escaping the media in the quiet countryside.

It was quite common for small groups, pairs or single young people to holiday on the camp site, some escaping the boundaries set by parents, some seeking fun with friends, and some searching for new relationships that could be dismissed and forgotten upon their return home. It was apparent that groups of young ladies outnumbered the groups of lads that chose to holiday in a rural campsite near the seaside and popular beaches. Bob and I always managed to bring smiles to their faces as we mowed around their caravans with genial banter, the girls considered us no threat to their reputation as they mainly comprised of girls in their late teens or early twenties, way too young to be worried about two old grass cutters sweating profusely and red faced and panting in exhaustion rather than sexual desire.

These sights became quite common and mostly went unnoticed as Bob and I went about our business, however it was not always so. The first day Bob attended the campsite, he discovered so many distractions that concentrating on the job proved difficult. On one occasion Bob rounded a caravan while also trying to control the old Hayter mower which had proved excellent for this type of work. Suddenly before him Bob encountered two young ladies lying on the grass enjoying the warm summer sunshine on their gently sweating bodies. The ladies obviously wanted a complete tan as there they lay, topless!

Wearing nothing but skimpy bikini bottoms and knowing smiles as they soaked up the sun, and the many admiring glances from male campers along with the envious stares from the female campers. No one commented or complained about the blatant nudity of the two prone young women, however one could hear the occasional click from a camera or the sharp sound of a slap as a husband or boyfriend peered too long or too closely at the girls.

I was just a few yards from Bob when I heard his abrupt exclamation and looked up to see what had caused the outburst. Noticing the two girls bathing flat on their backs in the bright sunlight I understood his reaction, however I did not expect his next action. With a flushed red face, Bob attempted to swing the mower away from the prone girls, pushing the roaring machine up hill in an attempt to avoid mincing those perfect bodies in front of him. By now I was almost parallel to Bob, keeping a suitable distance between the girls and the flying blades of my mower. It was part of the contact with the camp site that we did not disturb any of the campers. We had been instructed to mow around parked cars, littered possessions or persons sitting or lying or actively embracing each other on the grass outside their caravan, chalet or tent. Most people did in fact move as we neared their location, happy to allow us space to do our job and ensure the area was trimmed for their benefit. Of course there were always those who would simply watch us struggle round their cars or bodies without a thought of moving, but most campers were happy to move aside. The two girls however, had no intention of moving, they were enjoying themselves and the scene they were centred at. So both Bob and I were forced to circle round them at a distance safe from our mowers and any debris that may be thrown up by the actions of the machines.

Unfortunately Bob had not noticed their still and shapely bodies lying prone on the grass until he rounded the corner of the caravan. His exclamation and rapid reactions saved the girls from becoming sun baked mincemeat but caused him to lose his footing on the slippery grass. Pushing the mower hard up and away from the uncaring sun worshippers, Bob slipped. Giving the mower a mighty push as he fell forward, Bob sprawled onto the ground with a curse. Within a moment Bob was trying to regain his feet, but the forward motion of the mower had ceased and it was now already rolling back towards him. All the campers within sight had paused whatever they were doing to watch the spectacle, some in horror as they realised what was about to happen, others in anticipation of the resulting blood and gore. Bob desperately attempted to roll away from the lethal mower as I stopped my machine and leaped to his rescue. I was only a matter of feet away and I was able to grasp the handles of the menacing maniacal mower and halt its attack on Bob. Quickly I shut the motor down and repositioned the mower safely so it would not run away again, then I turned my attention to Bob in order to check his state of health. I need not have worried. There on the grass, lying between the two shocked young ladies was a beaming Bob! In his haste to avoid the run away mower, he had rolled completely over one girl and ended up sandwiched between their lithe young bronzed bodies. Bob appeared unhurt and very reluctant to move from his prone position and was grinning inanely at the applause directed at him from all the males who had witnessed the scene. With a sense of relief, I was pleased that my gardening colleague Bob had not suffered a major accident with the mower. I had no wish to attend his com-post mortem.

The two girls however were not so amused, their day of peacefully soaking up the sunshine and the appreciation of passing male campers and staff alike, had been shattered by the arrival of a sweaty, grass covered man in a most unseemly manner. Words that should never be heard from such beautiful ladies issued forth from their painted lips as they both strived to distance themselves from the grimy thirty something man lying in their midst. Finally Bob relented and with an exaggerated bow to his audience, he slowly rose from between the wriggling girls, taking great care where he placed his hands as he stood. Almost as soon as Bob had pried himself away, both girls hurriedly grabbed their towels and shot off into their caravan with blushes that out shone their tans.

Of course this episode was related to all who would listen for years and Bob's initial embarrassment soon developed in pride and he himself began telling the story, though his version had several embellishments.

Chapter Four: Celebrity Client

My small business of Green Fingers continued to survive and even prosper as new customers appeared almost daily. Our escapades at the campsite were all but forgotten and now we maintained the site on a regular fortnightly basis without further mishap. The diversity of the individual campers and their antics while in holiday mode provided us with a good deal of entertainment while we worked, and some of the sights we saw still managed to surprise us but few caused such an interesting reaction as that of the two sunbathing girls. Bob had settled down into the job and I rarely had to give him instructions or corrections, we were now operating like a well oiled machine.

Due to the success of the past weeks, I had invested in more equipment so the strenuous task of maintaining the campsite became a fraction easier, not much but enough to ensure we no longer dreaded the fortnightly battle with campers, vehicles, animals running loose and hyperactive kids tearing across in front of our mowers like Kamikaze pilots on wacky baccy. The addition of a self propelled mower certainly helped with the long uphill slopes of the central green and the playing areas though we still had to manually fight around the chalets, caravans and tents with the smaller machines.

The tented area created its own difficulties as people are inclined to leave items and possessions lying upon the grass, unseen by a sweaty gardener simply trying to get the job done as quickly and painlessly as possible. It often came as quite a shock to suddenly hear the mower squealing like a pig as once again a hidden dog toy was chewed in the mechanical mouth of the mower before being spat out in disgust. Worse still was the crunching sound as discarded beer bottles crashed against the mower blades and were flung out like confetti over the grass, which of course we had to clear for safety reasons. The beer bellied drinker responsible for the litter invariably never offered assistance but calmly opened another brown bottle before sucking greedily at its neck. The beer drinker appeared quite happy to watch us grope around on our hands and knees as we attempted to find and remove all traces of broken glass lying in wait for the unwary camper with bare feet, or the unwitting sun worshiper with an assortment of bare areas to attack.

Our efforts to remain calm and collected with only minor bouts of hysteria soon began to show benefit. The campsite owner had recommended our work to some of his friends and colleagues and in due course, more work began to flow in. One such recommendation followed a mysterious phone call late one Sunday evening. The gentleman on the phone wanted some work done to his lawns, he had three of them he said and they were all in need of attention. I assured him that my firm could handle the challenge and asked for his name and address. A silence followed, I checked to ascertain he was still on the other end of the line and he then replied. He gave a name, I say a name because I was sure it was not his real one, instead I gained the impression he was using an alias. Now this is a tad dodgy I thought, why would he not want to give his real name when seeking work to be undertaken on his property. My lack of enthusiasm must have been evident in my voice as I tried to hide my misgivings. Quickly he referred to the campsite owner as a reference, obviously attempting to calm my fears and obtain my services. Fine I thought, I will make him an appointment and reassess the situation when I attend his address. If I see one sign of villainy, suspicious behaviour or discover he is a closet politician, I will vacate his premises with all due haste. Thinking with my business head on, I also made a mental note to seek payment for any work done in cash, just in case.

On the allotted day we arrived in his small hamlet and being totally lost, I sought directions from an elderly man who was busy painting his garden wall. When I mentioned the name of the potential client, the elderly gents face clouded with confusion for a brief moment, then realisation penetrated his mind and with a huge grin he stated that I meant a person widely known under another name. Well of course I was very familiar with the name given by the elderly gent but hid my surprise and I repeated my request for directions. Still grinning the man indicated that we were only yards from our destination and pointed to a narrow lane up hill from where we stood. He then gave directions which appeared to be simple enough so with muttered thanks we set off in search of the location.

Moments later we arrived outside the property and we were greeted by a large and very familiar figure with a huge smile on his face as he held out his hand in welcome. I will not mention the stage name of the person as he may be embarrassed or annoyed with my story of the events, so I will give him yet another name and call him Mister Music. Obviously with a name like that one would quickly realise the nature of his business and I remember him reaching the number one spot in the British record charts during the seventies I think. I also remembered him from certain television programmes so to say he was well know would be some what of an under statement. Bob however, had no idea who Mister Music was and even when I later informed him of the famous songs and television programmes, Bob remained unconvinced, until I resorted to playing the most famous of Mister Music's songs on my van stereo later that day.

Back at the front gate, Mister Music invited us in and immediately asked if we wished some refreshments. I thanked him and answered that we did not but could we see the lawns that required attention. Still talking politely about his garden and the task ahead, Mister Music led us through the gate and past the back of his cottage. A large and friendly Golden Labrador came dashing out to meet us, followed by an attractive woman in an apron. With due fuss for the dog and introductions to his wife, Mister Music continued making his way to the rear of the cottage. There we found some steps running parallel to a tall wild looking hedge that lead up a steep slope to what he informed us was the first of his lawns.

Well! My mouth gapped and both Bob and I were at a total loss for words. Off on the left of the steps was a levelled area of total abandon. With the wild hedge on our right and the mountain of untamed vegetation on our left, I began to feel extremely claustrophobic. The so called lawn was a mass of brambles, thorny branches that had grown to enormous lengths and bowed over to form a prickly arch, but there were thousands of these branches shooting up from every square inch of the ground, not a blade of grass could be seen amongst the head high tangle of thorny branches. Neither Bob nor I were of tall stature but Mister Music appeared to be over six foot tall and even he could walk under the cave like snarl of brambles. Clumps of Dock leaves clustered around the outer edges of the brambles before a barrier of trees and ancient grass covering a stone hedge completed the trap. The area covered was approximately twenty foot wide and twenty two foot long. It was darkened further by over hung low branches from deciduous trees that added to the impression of impenetrable jungle.

'This is the first lawn,' he stated with a gesture, 'sorry its in such a state but that's why I called you boys in.'

'Lawn?' I questioned in shock, 'surely this has never been a *lawn*?'

'Yep I'm afraid it is a lawn, though I've not had the time to cut the grass for a few years and its gotten slightly out of hand. It shouldn't take much to put it right, hopefully?' Mr Music replied with a limp smile at our disbelieving faces. 'Anyway, let me show you the next two lawns. Please mind your heads as the way is somewhat difficult.'

His warning was understated as we mounted more steps bordered by the increasingly protruding hedge that lead up from the disaster of lawn number one and headed towards number two. Brambles and nettles fought to block our way to such an extent that I had to send Bob back to my van for hand scythes, branch loppers and a small saw so we could continue our battle onwards. Thus with slash of scythe and cut of saw we eventually discovered the second area that Mr Music alleged was a lawn. This too lead off to the left of the steps and, from what little we could see, also measured twenty foot by twenty two foot, the same as the first, and was in a similar state of confusion as lawn number one. But the journey did not end there; once again Mr Music forced his way further up the steps until he reached a large level area at the top of the steps and announced this was lawn number three. The steps and hedge came to a halt here so at least we could now see some blue sky above us. We had climbed about twenty feet up from lawn number one and as we cast our gaze about us, our immediate landscape resembled a huge brier patch. So much so that I half expected Brer Rabbit to flit in and out of the thorns, pursued by Brer Fox while Uncle Remus watched in amusement.

'This is lawn number three,' declared Mr Music with a wide gesture of his hands. 'This is where we like to entertain friends and hold barbecues during the summer when ever I can get away from work.'

'You've obviously not had a barbecue for some time, judging from the condition of your lawn.' I commented while trying to peer into the mass of over grown vegetation in order to gain some idea of the area involved.

'But I suppose you're not down in this part of the world too often, with your profession and all?'

'Not recently, no. But in answer to your second question, we do try to spend as much time here as work allows,' replied Mr Music. 'We hope to have some people down from London staying over next month and would like to be able to use all three lawns as soon as possible. What do you think?'

'Okay – Ah . . . Well Mr Music, lets be honest here, I believe you are friends with the nearby campsite owner?' I asked.

'Yes I am, I've known the guy for years and we often have a few drinks in the campsite bar when I'm home, for medicinal purposes you understand. Why do you ask?'

'No offence but if I can offer an honest opinion, may I suggest your friends stay at the campsite and you entertain them there. This garden is going to be a nightmare and will certainly not be fit for use this year at least.'

'Bugger! I was afraid of that,' muttered Mr Music with a downcast expression. 'Ah well, it can't be helped but it needs to be done anyway. Would you like to take on the job or is it only suitable for a JCB?'

'Well we can certainly return your lawns to grass but, it's going to take a while and of course the bill will reflect this. So what are your thoughts, are you still prepared to go ahead with the work?' I asked.

I was staring unhappily at the profusion of brambles, nettles, tall weeds and overhanging tree branches that our possible client described as lawns, I did not even consider the added complications of steep steps and possible snakes, pygmies and other assorted nasties that may lay hidden in the undergrowth. After some negotiating about the final cost and the fact that in reality a time period could not be set, Mr Music agreed to the expense and I agreed to undertake the work, though I admit my reluctance may have been evident in the apprehensive glances I threw at the terraces of jungle that Mr Music insisted on calling lawns.

The work began one cold and bright morning. In my van I had managed to procure an assortment of equipment and tools I deemed necessary for our expedition into the depths of tangled thorns Mr Music described as lawns. Parking as close as possible to the gate we began unloading the chainsaw, brush cutting strimmer, petrol hedge trimmer, two pairs of shears, branch loppers, safety goggles and two pairs of strong leather gloves. We were ready for battle!

It was obvious that some form of strategy was required in order to accomplish the task and to ensure we were not ripped to shreds. Everyone who has ever tackled brambles before will know of their uncanny ability to prick, cut and stab at all parts of ones body, seeming to move when one is unaware and wrap a thorny branch around a leg, arm or throat. Looking thoughtfully at the towering mass of chaos, we finally decided upon a full frontal attack as that was really the only option we had, attacking from the rear or using flaking tactics or even a charge of the Light Brigade were out of the question. Wielding hedge trimmer and shears Bob and I wadded in, whacking, slashing, cutting and sawing, we eventually managed to clear the offending brambles from the steps to allow us room to manoeuvre, or seek escape if the vegetation proved to be too formidable an opponent. Reaching our first objective which was the entrance to the lawn, we pushed forward into the razor filled mouth of the beast. Soon we were hacking away in abundance, forcing our way into the brambles inch by inch.

Until now most of our gardening work had been consumed with mowing grass and maintaining flower beds and borders, so we were not physically familiar with the hard labour involved in clearing such a profusion of brambles. We sweated and gasped in the claustrophobic airless stronghold of vicious vegetation that fought back against as and strove to slice and dice us like human sushi. Hacking down a clump of brambles at a time, we then managed to stomp the debris into a ball that could be stabbed with a fork and set aside for burning as soon as we had cleared enough space. Insects attacked us at every moment, thorns grabbed at us and the sun now burned brightly in the sky, its heat adding to our discomfort which slowly but surly began to be announced to the world in general as we gave vent to our frustration and pain. We had only gained a few feet into the tangle when a voice called from behind us but at first the new sound did not penetrate our thoroughly aggravated brains.

'Hello, would you like some refreshments? Whoa steady on, I'm right behind you!' A female voice shouted above the sounds of hacking, slashing and swearing.

Swinging round in the limited clear space I discovered Mrs Music standing apprehensively on the steps beside the area of destruction we were battling. Her blond hair flowed down across her shoulders, nicely decorated with scraps of amputated vegetation that flew in all directions as a result of mine and Bob's exertions. A bright pinny clung to her shapely figure and protected her light coloured jumper and pale blue jeans, a smile on her face concluded the vision of our rescuer as she gestured that we should follow her down the steps.

Quickly and with no reluctance we threw our tools down to the ground and eagerly succeeded her, emotions of relief and escape clearly showing on our grimy, sweaty blood streaked faces. Down the steps we trod, dodging stray branches, nettles and thorns that stretched out from the hedge in an attempt to ensnare us. I glanced in anger at the offending protrusions and made a mental note to hack the hell out of them when I returned, see how they liked it. Muttering obscenities under my breath I failed to notice several brambles lying in ambush across on of the steps. Suddenly my foot caught and I fell forward with a small cry, straight into the back of Bob who was walking down the steps in front of me. The result of this action saw both Bob and me arriving at the bottom of the steps in a very undignified heap. Most embarrassing for two grown men who were desperately trying to maintain an air of professionalism as we finally came to rest at the feet of Mr Music.

'Are you OK?' he enquired as he held out a helpful hand to assist our ascent from the hard path.

Peering up at the large smiling man above us, I tried hard to diminish the realisation that we must have looked like a right pair of plonker's lying dirty, sweaty and tangled at the feet of a famous person, a celebrity much loved by many and held in high esteem by his peers. We quickly assured him we were indeed unhurt as we brushed ourselves down before staring in astonishment at the refreshments offered. There in front of us on a small table sat a huge tray piled high with sausage rolls, pies, sandwiches, crisps and even vol-au-vents. To one side of the stacked tray were two large tea pots, a jug of milk, a bowl of sugar and four mugs. On the other side of the tray were plates and cutlery. A pure vision of delight reflected in our eyes as we stared at the feast in front of us.

'I hope you're hungry, I expect you are so I've prepared a small snack for you. If it's not enough I can do some more,' said Mrs Music.

'No, no I think there's plenty. Thank you very much,' I stammered in surprise.

Bob said nothing, I believe he was even dribbling slightly at the sight of so much food laid out before him, his stomach however did not remain silent and a clearly audible rumble issued forth as if in reply to her offer. With a reddening face Bob quickly held one hand against his stomach while accepting a plate from Mr Music with his other hand.

'Help yourselves,' he said with a smile, 'as you can see, my wife likes to ensure everyone is well fed.'

'Thank you. That looks delicious but there was no need as we both brought our packed lunches. Not as good as what you have there though so thank you again,' I replied as I reached out to grasp the first of many sausage rolls.

With heaped plates we all manoeuvred into position on the low garden wall and sat down to enjoy our selection of goodies. The dog joined us with wagging tail and huge begging brown eyes, unsure whether to seek attention from this gathering of humans, or to beg for food from who ever could be persuaded into parting with some scraps. Once the first few mouthfuls had been consumed and the greed in our stomachs had declined, we began the chore of small talk. I asked Mr Music if he was still working in the music and television business which initiated a conversation between all four of us on the fickle nature of the media and how hard it was to survive in such a business. I kept my replies and comments sympathetic while enviously pondering on the pitiful problems of being rich and famous. The talk continued onto what Mr Music was doing at the moment and he told us he had given up the television life in favour of his music, and that he was now very active on the folk music scene. I was delighted with this news, I had always been a fan of his music but not so his television programmes. Admittedly the programmes were intended for children but still I did not like them much, nor did my kids actually. Mr Music was a pleasant conversationalist and listener and the exchange was filled with humour and interest. His wife also proved to be an excellent host and contributed greatly to the conversation into which Bob and I added our contributions between mouthfuls of her savoury delights and mugs of tea.

Alas however time moved on and we had to return to the nightmare of Mother Nature and her vicious army of thorns, nettles and biting insects. To our surprise, Mr Music rolled up his sleeves and revealing strong brown forearms stated his intention of assisting us in our task, thus all three of us began mounting the steps towards our enemy as a soldier strides into war. But our enemy was waiting and well prepared for our onslaught, within minutes we were all bleeding from numerous stabs, pricks, cuts and slashes. I admit we were not injured to the extent of needing medical assistance, but it still hurt like hell every time the damned thorns struck home. However onward we strove, until we had cleared enough space to begin burning the bundles of brambles and other offending weeds without roasting ourselves in the process. Mr Music gratefully took on the task of pyromaniac and quickly disappeared in search of matches or similar incendiary devices. Some time passed before he returned with the news that, as non smokers, neither he nor his wife had any matches or a lighter or any other form of initiating combustion. I knew I had no such items either so I looked to Bob who did still enjoy the odd cigarette, only to find him frantically thumbing the striker wheel on what was evidently an empty lighter.

There followed a scene suitable for any television comedy show as three grown men stood in a circle around a heap of amputated bramble stems and scratched heads and rubbed chins thoughtfully. It was necessary to remove the cut vegetation piles in order to obtain space in which to work and of course to clear the debris in preparation for reseeding, so the problem had to be solved. Finally Bob came up with the only possible solution to our predicament.

'Umm, how about the cigarette lighter in the van?

'That won't work, the damn thing won't stay hot enough to melt butter by the time I've fetched it from the van all the way up here. We need a better idea,' I replied all too quickly.

'Nah I don't mean bring the lighter all the way up here. All we have to do is light a taper or rolled up newspaper, that should give us enough time to get back up here before burning our hands off or the flame goes out.' stated Bob in an exasperated tone.

Mr Music and I looked at each other in comprehension, 'Yep that'll work,' I said after receiving an acknowledging nod from the client.

'Anyone got a newspaper or something similar?

Obviously neither I nor Bob had anything combustible upon our person so Mr Music set off once again to obtain burnable material from his abode. I followed him down the steps and went out to my van in order to warm up the vehicle cigarette lighter with a furtive prayer that the damn thing would work. I had only owned the van for a month or two and so far the need to use the lighter had not arisen. Opening the passenger door I jumped into the van and pushed in the small round head of the lighter and held my breath in hope that it would actually work. After about thirty seconds I could breathe again as the lighter popped out, signifying it was hot, least I hoped it was. Pulling it from its holder I was relived to see the element inside glowing a bright red, it worked. Now man had fire! Thankfully I reinserted the lighter into its port and awaited the arrival of Mr Music with something I could ignite. Within moments he appeared with a rolled up sheet of newspaper so I pushed the lighter in once more to reheat it. When done I wrenched it from its socket and offered it up the paper held in Mr Music huge hand. The paper quickly ignited and off he set, hurrying back to the steps and up towards the first lawn and the vegetation sacrifice, a soon to be burnt offering to

Mother Nature herself. I quickly replaced the lighter, locked the van and followed Mr Music round the back of his cottage and rushed to the steps.

Unfortunately the steps themselves were of amateur construction and were not entirely level or evenly spaced, so it was not surprising that half way up the steps towards lawn number one, Mr Music tripped. In his haste he had missed his footing and began to fall forward. As he descended towards the hard and unwelcoming steps, Mr Music threw the flaming roll of paper out to one side so he would not burn himself by landing on the burning issues of the day. The flaming newspaper shot from his hand and landed with a burst of sparks at the base of the overgrown hedge that bordered the steps. Within seconds the hedge began to burn. Not exactly what we intended. With a shout to Bob I ran up and attempted to stamp out the flames with my foot, but alas to no avail and the flames licked higher up the hedge with a bright yellow glee.

Mr Music was already back on his feet and running frantically down the steps once more while shouting to his wife to fill a bucket of water. Bob had now joined me and like rabid Morris Dancers we both stomped and stamped at the flames in an attempt to put out the fire at ground level. No way was I even considering those flames that flickered higher than my knee caps; after all I am not a contortionist. From the cottage we could hear the shouted confusion as Mr and Mrs Music fought to fill buckets, bowls and pans with water as swiftly as humanly possible. Moments later up the steps flew the couple, armed now with containers full of splashing water. With a heave, Mr Music threw his water at the flaming hedge, only managing to thoroughly soak me with the entire contents of the bucket. Screaming at him to get more water and be more careful, Mrs Music came forth with her container and carefully poured its contents over the base of the fire.

Bob and I had finished our attempts at maniacal dancing and followed Mr Music down to the cottage to obtain more water. With a sudden flash of intelligence I shouted for everyone to form a chain as there was simply not enough room on the narrow steps for us to pass each other safely. So in the order in which we found ourselves, we began a sort of fire chain. Mr Music filled the containers and passed them to me waiting outside her kitchen, I then ran to the bottom of the steps only a few paces away and handed said container to Bob. Bob then carefully mounted the steps and handed the water container to Mrs Music who then threw the water upon the fire. Once empty, Mrs Music passed the container back to Bob, who in his own definition of wisdom threw the container down the steps to me. This was fine at first, until I was faced on one side with a container brimming full of water and on the other side an empty container is flying through the air towards me, having been thrown by the ever intellectual Bob. To be honest I made no heroic leaps or acrobatics in an attempt to catch both the containers directed at me, I simply ducked. The empty container flew over my head and hit Mr Music on his shoulder which caused him to react by throwing his bowl full of water forward, all over me once again!

Finally the fire was extinguished and we sat wherever we stopped and sought to catch our breath. I was sopping wet from both my drenches but sweat from my exertions and the warm sun combined to make the experience of being wet quite pleasurable. Puffing and panting we gathered up all the containers and made our way down to the cottage where Mrs Music had decreed we could rest and have a hot cup of tea. I was very pleased to hear this offer; I did not really want a cold cup of tea . . .

Eventually we recovered so Mr Music, Bob and I set off up the steps again to continue clearing the brambles and unwanted vegetation from the area amusingly described as a lawn. We had only gone a few steps when I noticed tucked away beside the hedge was a garden hose pipe attached to a water tap. Turning to face Mr Music I pointed at the tap and raised an eyebrow in question.

'Dammit! In all the panic I'd forgotten that tap. Oh well, the fires out so no use complaining over spilt water.'

Reaching our destination we glanced around and assessed what stage of the demolition we were before becoming improvised firemen. It was at that moment I realised with some despondency that with all the fire raging about us, no one had thought to obtain a light and ignite the heap of brambles that had started the whole fiasco! Once again I set off still dripping towards my van and its cigarette lighter while Mr Music headed off to obtain more newspaper. Bob simply sat upon a space of cleared ground and howled with laughter at the absurd situation. I was not so amused and vowed to get my revenge at the earliest opportunity.

This time the plan worked well, Mr Music took care as he mounted the steps once more with the flaming roll of paper held out in front of him. Bob had also secured a few pages from the newspaper and had tucked them under the brambles at the base of the heap. One stab into that paper with the burning brand caused the heap to immediately combust, resulting in a healthy fire within moments. As I was still wet and I think Mr Music felt guilty, as he should. I was allowed to maintain the fire while Mr Music and Bob launched into the fray once again and began hacking at the cathedral of brambles as I slowly steamed dry.

At last lawn number One was cleared and we hacked our way up to lawn number Two. With knowledge gained from the previous bramble battle we attacked the second lawn with experience. The fire still burned happily on lawn One so we simply threw the bundles of slashed and amputated thorns and weeds over the edge of the second lawn, and down to the fire some six feet below us. Each of the three lawns was terraced at approximately six to seven feet between stages, slate and granite stones formed retaining walls which supported each of the three lawns.

Work progressed happily amidst the heat from the sun, the eye watering smoke that arose from the fire, the cuts, stabs and stings from the savage vegetation and the bits from the hordes of insects that had descended on us with a feast in mind. I had mostly dried out from my double soaking, but to be honest I was sweating so much I could no longer differentiate between genuine water or sweat soaked clothing. I was happily surprise at the amount of effort Mr Music contributed to the task of bramble extermination. I suppose one always assumes celebrities are soft pampered weaklings, Mr Music proved the contrary. Standing alongside Bob and me, Mr Music worked furiously in his battle to rediscover his lost lawns, sweat and blood stained his clothing as he swung the hand scythes with gusto, often causing both myself and Bob to hurriedly duck under the flashing path of the curved blade. I remember pondering on Mr Music's repeated pleas of '*Sorry*' whenever the scythe flew dangerously close to our heads, I wondered would the word sorry suffice when presented with a headless gardener flopping like a fish upon the ground.

However the work progressed and three days later all three lawns were bare of vegetation. Obviously reseeding would be necessary but at least Mr Music now had three empty spaces he could reclaim as lawns. Bob and I had enjoyed our time with Mr and Mrs Music; in fact I swear I gained a couple of pounds in weight thanks to the trays of delicious food presented to us twice a day by Mrs Music, who I must add was a great cook. Mr Music had regaled us with humorous tales from the show business world and kept us entertained during tea breaks. I did try and persuade him to play a few songs but he politely refused, I understood as music was his job - his work. When not involved in his chosen profession he avoided picking up his guitar or singing, he took a break from work in other words. I wish I could have convinced my dear wife of this fact, designing, shaping and maintaining gardens all week as a form of employment did not induce me to spending my weekends gardening at home!

Chapter Six: Snakes alive.

Now I must confess I am no hero, working at the cemetery was creepy enough but dealing with unsuspected wild life proved an even bigger strain on my old bladder. My landscaping company, which at that time was me and Bob, had been hired to maintain a large private garden that consisted of two massive lawns, an orchard and several tree and shrub areas. The grounds and its accompanying house had originally been built as a gate keeper's home and was situated at the main entrance to what was formerly a grand estate. Who ever owned the estate and the manor house had spent lavishly on the gate keeper's house, it was not a small two up, two down cottage as is normally the case. Instead it had the appearance of being built in the same style as the manor but on a much smaller scale. It owned four bedrooms where as the manor had in the region of twenty or more I believe. It possessed a small cobbled court yard just off the long stately drive that lead, eventually to the manor, and it was surrounded by the fields, lawns and manicured gardens that once belonged, alone with the gate keeper's house and garden, to the owner of the manor.

These days the manor was a holiday park and
the Gate House along with the fore mentioned grounds
had been divided off and sold. The Gate House was now
occupied by a couple with two teenage daughters. The
husband served in one of the British armed forces while
the wife ran a small business from home. Both the girls
were of school age, I knew that because I recognised
their school uniforms. But as to their age I had not a
clue however I would estimate approximately that one
was approaching school leaving age with the other not
far behind her. I stated approximately because in
today's modern and liberated world, no one can
accurately judge the age of a young girl any more, and I
was no different. As far as I was concerned, neither girl
sported pigtails or carried dolls, nor did either have
wrinkles or greying hair. They were young girls often
dressed in the fashion of that period, and looked to me
just like any other girls aged between twelve and
twenty. I realise this description of the younger
generation suggests that I was a tad older than the two
girls and this would be correct. At that time I think I
was in my early thirties, a truly ancient age in the eyes
of teenagers.

In truth we did not see much of the girls or the
father in the duration of our time at the gate house; in

fact we rarely even saw the wife as all the family appeared to have quite busy lives. This suited me as we could get on with our work without any customer distractions. Whenever we did stumble across a member of the family lurking in the bushes or quietly appearing round a corner of the house we were met with politeness and pleasantries, each of the family being extremely well mannered. This took some getting used to as both Bob and I were more accustomed to being growled at by our customers as they issued their desired instruction for the day. Through our infrequent chats and even more sporadic offers of refreshment in the form of tea, coffee or a cold drink, I eventually discovered the family had not long moved into the Gate House and were only renting with an option to buy at a later stage. I received the impression that actually buying the Gate House was out of the question, no matter how long they chose to live there, for the market price of such a luxurious property would be prohibitive to the ordinary working class people. However they were happy with the house, its vast gardens, location and hopefully, the pair of nondescript layabouts that cheekily entitled themselves as gardeners.

We had been employed on an hourly basis, consisting of two hours every fortnight for several months before discovering any excitement at the Gate House, and it certainly was not in the form we had both hoped for. Summer was in its infancy with pleasantly warm days and plenty of sunshine. This was a complete shock to us as like all British people, we retreat into withdrawal when our days fail to bring the expected and accepted rain. However we clenched our teeth and dutifully forced our astonished minds and bodies to strive on regardless. The work necessary to maintain the grounds of the Gate House in only two hours per fortnight kept Bob and I constantly rushing round trying to catch our tails. The two large lawns first had to have the edges trimmed with a strimmer and edging irons, stray branches, vagrant stones, pet toys and wandering minstrels all had to be cleared from the lawns in preparation for mowing. The mowing of each lawn took a substantial chunk from our allotted schedule. So by the time we arrived at the orchard we were cursing the day we became gardeners and praising those with the foresight to have artificial turf laid instead of grass, or even concrete.

The orchard presented its own difficulties, each tree had to be avoided by the mowers, no mean feat for Bob as he constantly forgot to check where he was walking and frequent profanities ripped through the quietness of the day as he blindly walked straight into yet another tree. Manoeuvring around the closely planted apple trees, dodging low hanging branches, kamikaze squirrels and odd discarded tree limb proved quite a task for Bob. He was more of a straight line sort of guy, if it was green and in front of him, he would cut it. However too many obstacles swiftly became a strain on Bob's working routine, finesse was certainly not his forte.

At the far end of the orchard was a small clearing which had been used for decades as a dumping ground for garden waste and debris and resembled a small mountain jutting up from the grass and covering an area of twenty five square yards, each side being about five yards long. The compost heap reached a height of approximately five to six foot and was entirely covered in stinging nettles. I have described it as a compost heap for want of a better description. In truth it was simply an unused area within the grounds where decades of gardeners had dumped grass cuttings, weeds, branches and any other debris. I doubt if any of the material there could be used as compost but that is the word I will use for the moment. Off to the left some ten yards away stood a dilapidated shed in the twilight of its life, a long unused potting table stood alongside the shed standing as a silent sentinel over the up turned wheel barrow and scattered garden implements and empty flower pots. Situated a short distance from the shed stood a forlorn greenhouse, its glass green and stained, weeds grew in profusion both inside and out, portraying evidence that it, like the shed, had not been in use for many years. Our instructions were to ignore this section of the garden because the family had no desire to resurrect these monuments to a past gardening glory. However we did have to mow around the compost heap in order to allow access for further grass cuttings and assorted detritus that all gardens produce. It was here that we, or more specifically me, received a fright to surpass that of the cemetery.

As I have already stated, I am no hero however I do not fear the average wildlife inhabitant of the British Isles. Let's face it; we do not have wolves, bears, lions, tigers, Yeti, unicorns, or other assorted nasty type animals roaming the green and pleasant lands of this Emerald Isle. We do not have to avoid elk, moose, wild haggis or rampant water buffalo when strolling through the countryside, or even our towns. We live in a relatively safe country with only teenage motor vehicle drivers, door to door salesmen and the odd feisty pensioner to provide a stimulating hazard to our otherwise peaceful lives. However the British wildlife does include three forms of that slippery reptile, the snake.

Three species of snake inhabit the United Kingdom, first the well known Grass snake (*Natrix natrix*), a harmless reptile often found in open woodlands, gardens and hedgerows. Next comes the rarer Smooth snake (*Coronella austriaca*), uncommon and mostly limited to heathland. Finally there is Britain's one and only poisonous snake, the Viper or Adder (*Vipera berus*), found all over the United Kingdom on heathland, open woodlands and commons. None of these snakes are casually seen in our countryside, each has the good sense to avoid humans and their heavy feet and discarded beer cans. Most shy away as soon as a noisy biped approaches so many folk in Britain today have never even seen one. I was to get my chance.

On one particular visit to the Gate House, the lady of the house asked if I would tidy the unsightly pile that nestled at the far reaches of her grounds, the same one I mentioned earlier. After some brief discussion it was decided that I would strim down all the stinging nettles and remove branches and any other combustible material to the bonfire site that was situated behind the dilapidated shed. I asked if she want the shed added to the fire but she declined. The compost heap she informed me, could be seen from the road and she did not want such an untidy area of her garden visible to those passing by, it lowered the tone of the area. I looked around at this statement. The one road in sight was that leading to the holiday camp and used mainly by travellers glued to their Satnavs in fear and confusion as they struggled to discover the advertised wonders of this secluded Holiday Park. Otherwise the whole area was surrounded by trees. No one who mattered could possibly offend their delicate eyes upon the hideous compost heap overgrown with nettles. However I was there to work and the task offered a couple more hours of work which in turn meant a few more coins in my pocket. I agreed.

Once I had finished my area of lawn, I collected the petrol strimmer (brush cutter) and headed off into the wildness in search of the ancient monument locally know as the *shed*, and the sacrificial mound otherwise known as the *compost heap*. The day itself was warm, quite warm in fact, my face leaked profusely under the insistent British sun and the world acquired a very strange cast as the blue of the sky blanketed the green of the foliage. Birds and animals panicked in the weird illumination of the day, like myself the animals and birds were more familiar with an overcast grey sky indigenous to the United Kingdom. Still I soldiered on, battling thirst as I had not enjoyed a delicious cup of tea for at least an hour. Bob was still plodding along behind his mower red faced and puffing, he paid me no attention as I staggered past. Finally I reached the untidy site of the compost heap with its nettles reaching to the sky. Placing the strimmer upon the ground I positioned my face guard on my head and rolled down my shirt sleeves before pulling thick protective gloves onto my hands. I had cut stinging nettles before and was well aware of the resulting painful nettle goo that stuck to ones bare flesh like a coat of biting insects.

At last I was ready. Steeling myself against the battle ahead I started my machine and set about the heap with gusto. I had barely cut a few feet into the nettles when something caught my eye. I immediately stopped cutting – suddenly the strimmer was flying through the air and I was running like a mad man away from the compost heap. Snake! I had seen a snake slithering through the area I had just cleared. I had not waited around long enough to notice that as I ran in one direction, the snake had wriggled off in the other direction. I did not care, fright, fear and brown underwear had attacked my very being and I fled.

Bob had surfaced from his automotive stupor long enough to witness my flight and rushed to my side to discover the reason behind my sudden burst of activity. As he reached me I stopped my foreword momentum and simply stood there bent over with my hands on my knees as I fought to overcome my fright and initiate breathing again.

'What the hell happened to you? What's the matter?' Bob enquired quickly.

'Puff, pant, gulp, wheeze . . . .' was my reply.

'Are you alright? What's up?' Bob asked again.

'Sss-snake!' I finally blurted out.

'What? What snake? What have you been drinking? There ain't any snakes here. And why are you bright red?' retorted Bob.

'It was a bleddy snake! It was right in front of me, I couldn't miss it. Over in the heap there.' I pointed shakily to the forest of nettles some hundred feet away.

'I saw a damn snake and it was bleddy huge!'

'Yeah right. What kind of snake then?' mocked Bob.

'I dunno. As soon as I saw it I legged it away. Bleddy snakes frighten the life outta me.' I gasped.

'Ok, ok calm down. Tell me what it looked like, you sure it wasn't just a big worm?' asked Bob.

'Of course it wasn't a flaming worm! It was . . , well the bit I actually saw was over three foot long and it looked like a silvery colour. But that was only half of the damn thing. I think the other end was already heading into the nettles. So if I only saw a part and it was about three inches thick, how long was the bugger? It must have been about six to eight foot long.' I explained.

'Nah,' replied Bob, 'I've never see a snake in the wild but I'm sure they ain't that long. You sure you saw a snake?'

I insisted that I had in words not appropriate to be included here and finished with the challenge; 'Why don't you go and have a bleddy look if you're such an expert?'

'I ain't going go over there,' he said, 'it might still be there.'

'I thought you didn't believe me? Don't tell me you're frightened of a snake?' I teased.

'Well you bloody well are!' he retorted.

'True but I'm the one who saw the damn thing, I don't need any reminding thank you very much.'

'But the customer wants that area cleared so you've gotta go back. Anyway I expect its long gone by now,' insisted Bob, 'it was probably more frightened of you anyway.'

'Don't think so some how. I certainly didn't see any signs of that bleddy huge snake messing himself when he saw me. In fact I'd bet the bugger was laughing at me.' I replied.

'Not surprised. The way you took off running would have made anyone laugh. The sight really brightened my day,' he laughed as he began to walk off towards his machine to carry on with the task in hand. This meant him simply finishing cutting the lawn, I on the other hand, still had to clear the heap and its slippery inhabitant. Great! Luckily it appeared the reptile had departed the vicinity and I never encountered it again. Bob of course never believed my story and blamed it on the unaccountably warm British weather.

My next encounter with the long thin members of the reptile species came from an even more unexpected location. I was working with Trev again and we were maintaining a small business on the outskirts of a local village. The business was relatively new and sold items hand crafted by locals to gullible holiday makers.

The building itself had once been a primary school, built in granite block and in the style of many English schools dating from the late 19th century. The solid grey granite walls were topped by grey slate and black iron guttering with dirty brown terracotta ridge tiles. A gothic arched door provided access in and out of the building and high arched windows supplied illumination. For those unfortunate to be old enough to remember, the sight of the building brought memories of cold classrooms, blackboards and chalk, very small bottles of lukewarm milk each morning and reciting the times table parrot fashion. Snotty noses, short trousers, nits, scabbed knees and a genuine fear of teachers, especially the head teacher who dealt out punishment that would result in a frenzied police ambush and a charge of assault today.

The grounds still included the small playground immediately behind the building but now its function was that of a car park. The lines painted on the tarmac dated from when children played football and other games on its surface. Surprisingly many customers to the car park assumed the faded white lines were a guide to parking. Often vehicles were left in a variety of positions as witless drivers attempted to park around the central ring of the former football pitch markings. Small lawns lined the entrance to the car park and business entrance on the right of the building. A further wall retained a hillock area of grass that fought against the onslaught of Japanese Knotweed (*Fallopia japonica, Polygonum cuspidatum, Reynoutria japonica*) at the rear of the building. Adjacent to this section stood a small area hidden behind shrubs and bushes and this was used for depositing the grass cuttings and as a bonfire site, safely hidden from the gaze of potential customers.

The work here was hard, the main stretches of grass that provided a boundary between the main road and the business was situated on a steep hill, which meant slogging up and down the hill for the entire length of the grounds. Certainly an excellent aerobic exercise if one wanted to look at such an activity in a positive manner. Rest assured we did not see the aerobic advantages of pushing a heavy petrol mower up the incline repeatedly for an hour or more. Our views of the hundred or so yards of steep grass were mostly in the negative, aggravated further each time a large diesel fume spewing truck thundered past and polluted the air we were desperately trying to drag into our heaving lungs. As the business proprietor wanted the grounds to be as tidy as possible, we were requested to collect the grass cuttings in the mower boxes and empty them on the small cuttings pile in the hidden area behind the bushes. This was not a problem unless the damn box needed emptying when one was at the bottom of the hill. Then a long slog ensued, carrying the full grass box back up the hill, through the car park and up at another small slope to deposit the grass. I had maintained this venue for some years and knew to empty the grass box at the top of the hill, whether it needed it or not. This had become such a habit I virtually ran on automatic, though I do not mean *ran* in the true meaning of the word. However my laborious trip to and from the cuttings pile changed after this day.

The sun's heat bore down on me that day and the inclined section of grass that separated the Gallery from the main road grew steeper with each step as the hot roaring mower appeared to gain weight with every up hill struggle. I had been up and down this section several times before it became necessary to empty my grass box so I pulled it away from my machine and headed over to the cuttings pile. As I turned the corner around the screen of bushes, I could hear a strange sound, very much like a high pitched whistle. I stopped to listen for a moment as my hot brain tried to identify the sound and its origin. I failed, I had never heard such a sound before, but I realised it was quite near me. Finally the curiosity evaporated in the heat and I approached the pile, grass box at the ready. Suddenly I noticed the strange noise had become louder, and closer. Still choosing to ignore the sound, I looked down at the cuttings pile in readiness to empty the box and there curled up on top of the heap right in front of me was a snake! I only caught a brief glimpse of those brownish coils because within a split second I was off and running.

Panic subsided once I had reached what I deemed a safe distance from the reptile, I halted my dash and took stock of the situation. What on earth was I running from I wondered. It was not as if the snake was a cobra or rattlesnake because here in Britain the majority of our poisonous snakes work in banking or politics. The animal I had seen, though fleetingly was much too long to be a Viper and that conclusion left only two possibilities. However although my brain was now functioning logically, sadly my courage was not, so before returning to the pile I called on the support of Trev. Maybe not a wise decision but what choice did I have? I was certainly not brave enough to face the thing by myself.

Calling Trev over I explained what had
happened and suggested we take a look to see if it was
still there and ascertain what type of reptile it was. With
a shrug of his shoulders, Trev declared that he did not
fear snakes and asked: 'If it's still there, can we kill it?'

'Kill it? What the hell for? There's no reason to
kill it just because it frightened the crap outta me!' I
replied in surprise.

'That sounds like a pretty good reason to me,' he
said, 'I kill spiders and flies. I hate spiders.'

'No we're not going to harm the thing, providing
of course it doesn't go for us. If it does it's all yours
because I'll be way in the distance by then.'

And with that muttered statement of pure
honesty I led the way back to the grass cuttings pile.
Any logic I possessed was still being over-ridden by
primitive fear. So instead of rounding the shrubs we
choose to view the heap through a gap in the bushes,
visible above the remains of a three foot high stone wall
that surrounded the rear edge of the cuttings and rubbish
area. Slowly and very, very carefully we peered in
silence through the bushes, our bodies nearing the wall
as we strove to glimpse the snake without disturbing it,
or me. The cuttings heap was in clear view but of the
snake there was no sign. Disappointed, and very

relieved, I stood back just as Trev shouted. There on the ground coiled inches from our feet was the snake.

Before our flight of fright could begin, the snake itself took off. In an amazing display of agility it shot straight up the wall and disappeared through the bushes and into the Japanese Knotweed and weeds that encompassed the heap. From a coiled position right up against the foot of the wall, the snake has climbed three foot vertically and vanished. Now my reactions set in and I turned to flee, but as I turned I realised I was alone. My erstwhile unafraid and callous colleague was already sprinting away at great speed!

Moments later found us both locked securely in my van, sipping at hot tea held in shaking hands as we recovered from the scare. Once settled we reflected on what we had seen and pondered the choice of actions we should, or should not take. Even in my frightened state I had recognised the reptile as a harmless Grass Snake, it was approximately six foot long (*I may have exaggerated the length here*), mostly brown with bright yellow flashes behind its head. It is recorded that Grass snakes do not bite, they are not known to strangle, suffocate or even whip one with their tail, they do not even shout abuse, in fact about the only form of defence they use is to play dead. Well this begger did not, it was every active, so much so that it had disappeared before I could, though Trev had run a good race I concluded. As it was a warm summer, the thought finally occurred to us that the snake was nesting, if that is what one calls a snake coiled on a hot compost heap and refusing to vacate the area. So I dutifully reported the snake and its whereabouts to the proprietor, explaining that it may intimidate and possibly mug her customers. However the business owner was a kindly soul and ordered us to leave it alone, thankfully. Instead we were to discard any grass cuttings and other horticultural detritus in another area of the grounds so we would not disturb the mother Grass snake. I was very happy to oblige.

Our final encounter with an alleged snake came while Bob and I were trimming the tall hedge at the top of Mrs Wain's garden. Bob of course had not originated from the countryside; he was more familiar with city life where most of the *wild life* wore hoodies. He had little idea about our native creatures and hence became the butt of several practical jokes and tall tales. Over the course of time he had worked for me, I had managed to convince him that the common Slow Worm (*Anguis fragilis*) was indeed the more dangerous Viper, or Adder depending of ones choice of description. Mrs

Wain's property was a haven for these harmless legless lizard creatures with its small compost heap, dangerous things these compost heaps. There was also a shed that was raised up about two inches off the ground via blocks, and the rear granite wall was dry built. No cement or super glue had been used in its construction and so the wall, shed and compost heap provided many places in which a Slow Worm could hide.

We had seen several during our time visiting Mrs Wain's property and I had urged Bob to keep his distance from these nasty creatures. It worked; even when I relented and picked one up to move it from the path of our mower he would not believe a Slow Worm was harmless. In his mind, anything that had no legs and slithered was a snake. It was a situation just begging to be taken advantage of.

One this particular day Bob was using a pair of gardening shears tidying up those small branches and twigs not cut by the hedge trimmer, humming quietly to himself while I packed away the hedge cutter and cables. I normally used an electric hedge cutter for the domestic gardens as the petrol one was heavy and cumbersome, and I was lazy. Bob continued to inspect and trim the left over twigs happily, his back to me as he concentrated on the job in hand. An idea entered my normally empty head and with an evil grin I crept nearer to Bob. I stooped to pick up a long thin twig that had just a couple of small leaves still attached at one end as I moved quietly nearer. Bob was still engrossed in his work, still humming a little tune with no comprehension of my dastardly plan. When I was near enough, I silently reached forward and gently moved the tip of the twig against Bob's ankle while emitting a whispered hiss. The result was spectacular! Resembling an Olympic high jumper, Bob shot up into the air with a cry of horror. The shears were flung aside as he landed at a run, and sprinted off down the garden.

'What's up with you?' I shouted with a laugh.

'Bloody snake just bit me!' he wailed as he finally came to a panting halt.

'What snake?' I asked.

'One of those bloody adder things. I felt the bugger on me ankle. Watch it, it may still be there and it'll bite you if you're not careful,' he gasped in reply.

'Ah come on,' I said with mirth evident in my voice, 'there ain't any adders here. I told you there are only harmless Slow Worms here and they won't bite you. Beside I doubt they would like the taste.'

'I'm bloody telling you I felt summat bite me ankle!' he shouted as he bent down to gingerly examine his ankle.

'You sure it was a bite?' I asked.

'Course I'm bloody . . .' as he spoke, Bob looked up at me for the first time since attempting to clear the hedge in one bound, and realised I was slowly waving the twig at him.

'Ahh for f . . . bloody hell! It was you, you bastard!' he shouted at me as realisation dawned. 'What the hell did you do that for? I thought I was gonna bloody die!'

Off he stomped towards the van and refused to come out until I had apologised profusely and promised not to scare him like that ever again. I agreed once I had stopped laughing and eventually our normal routine was resumed. Bob however did not forget the incident, and obtained his revenge at a later date. That is another story and the telling may come later. The practical joke did have a positive benefit however. Bob finally overcame his fear of Slow Worms, and even took on the chore of clearing them from harms way when ever one attempted to metamorphose into mincemeat under our mowers. We never did see any Adders.

Chapter Seven: Cemetery.

Our work in the business sector was expanding just as much as the work for private customers and residents, with contracts coming in thick and fast, well; every now and then really. Along with the campsite we also gained one cemetery (*including occupants*), one storage company, a double glazing company and an art gallery. These jobs were profitable because it meant we were in one place doing one job for several hours instead of having to pack up and move on to another job at the end of an hour or two. Most of our residential clients only required our services for an hour or two a fortnight, so obviously much of our day was spent travelling from one location to another, even though I attempted to undertake as many jobs as possible within the same area each day. Unfortunately this did not happen too often, in fact other than businesses, we had but one housing estate where we had enough clients to justify a full days work. So any trade or business accounts were a blessing and boosted our coffers nicely, however the down side of business accounts was that they required me to send in a monthly bill and they would then hopefully send out a cheque at the end of each month. I realise this is a standard method of conducting business transactions, but it still felt to me like I was working for nothing when I completed each job but left with no actual cash in my pocket.

Amongst our new business customers we also had the delights of a couple of parish councils. Although it was often interesting work due to the variety of tasks they set us, getting bills settled became a real chore. It has been long understood that politicians talk for a living, be it parish council, town council, district council, county council or members of Parliament, they all waffle endlessly in their chosen career, and often just for fun apparently. However I did not expect the amount of waffling and time wasting when attempting to obtain payment for a job completed. The parish council in question had obviously agreed to hire our firm, they had agreed upon the nature of said job and even agreed on the amount they wished to pay, but when it came to actually settling the account, then suddenly no one could agree! I did eventually learn how to deal with this by submitting my bill two weeks before I actually did the work and I almost got paid on time. Amusingly, for all their talk, pomposity and arrogance, they never figured out what I was doing.

One such task we were set by a local town council involved the maintenance of their cemetery on a weekly basis during the summer months then as required throughout the remainder of the year. This is where I made another big mistake in my estimation of how long this particular job would take, a mistake I would regret in sweat for an entire season. When asked to undertake the maintenance of the cemetery I first visited the place as usual before offering a price. The cemetery was situated well out of the town, upon the side of a hill that had spectacular views over the valley and was locally known somewhat appropriately as Boot Hill, obviously. It was a delightful location chosen by someone who evidently intended the deceased to enjoy the beautiful panorama as they rested for eternity. Just as noticeably no land speculator or land agent or even a builder with an eye on profit had visited the site before the council of old had acquired it. Otherwise the location combined with the perfect views would have been littered with numerous and very expensive houses in no time at all. But for now the plot was owned by the local council and the dead, and as the residents of Boot Hill caused no disturbance or disruption to the community. No ghosts, vampires or zombies frightened or feasted upon the so called *human* inhabitants of the town, so everyone remained happy with the situation. Except of course for the builders, the estate agents and the land agents, who viewed the site with pound signs glittering in their greedy eyes!

The cemetery itself was divided into three sections. When entering through the large ornate wrought iron gates, one first encountered a tarmacadam access road or rather a wide pathway that stretched out in a 200 yard long straight line from the gates and across the entire length of the graveyard, ending abruptly at a tall hedge at the far side. Another access path angled off from the main one at ninety degrees and separated two sections on the right of the main access route. The section nearest the gates was full and the graves showed the cruel passage of time on the surfaces of the stones, faintly legible lettering upon the stones and plaques gave witness to the dates of the deceased, some dating back to the concluding years of the nineteenth century. The right hand section furthest from the gates was in its last stages of being full, new graves were evident at the far end, shaded by the hedge that marked the boundary of the cemetery.

A thin strip of undisturbed ground running parallel to the hedge showed the physical limit of the remaining free space. I use the term physical due to the proximity of the hedge which in truth was a line of trees, perhaps remaining from times past when the area

was completed covered in forest. No graves could be
dug in this strip of land due to the web of tree roots that
criss-cross through the soil, making penetration by
spade virtually impossible. Hand tools such as spades
and shovels have long been replaced in the armoury of a
grave digger by the modern mechanical mini diggers,
the mutant offspring of full sized bull dozers and yellow
diggers that now succeed the grave digger of old.
Certainly a mini digger in full roar could rip through the
soil unhampered by the maze of roots lying beneath, but
let's face it, who would want their deceased loved ones
bones being tangled in roots while they rested. Come to
think of it, having their roots cut, mangled and torn
asunder would not have pleased the trees either.

Finally a large area of grass stretched the length
of the cemetery on the left side of the main pathway.
This area was not divided and was still largely unused,
just a handful of graves had appeared over the most
recent years and were positioned at the far end near the
hedge border, otherwise this section was empty of
resting places. Except for moles! This otherwise healthy
section of lush green grass resembled a war zone, moles
hills littered the area like miniature mountains and pot
holes. And to make matters worse, the damn moles
appeared to be attracted to the sound and vibration

caused by our mowers as we fought our way through the grass. I will state here and now that we never actually minced any moles, though it was often quite a close shave.

But returning to the mistake I made, when pricing the work to be done at the cemetery I underestimated just how time consuming it would be to cut around headstones and assorted grave paraphernalia. *And avoiding kamikaze moles!* Not having any experience of graveyards I did what I always did and estimated the cost by size, I noted the size of the area to be mown, estimated the time required and arrived at my conclusion from that. I did add some extra just in case, however even that was not enough but having submitted a quote, I was stuffed, well and truly, just like a turkey at Christmas.

The day came of the first cemetery cut and Bob and I arrived at the crack of nine o'clock on a chill but bright morning. Dew sparkled on the grass and on ornaments decorating the graves, birds sang in the surrounding trees, moles popped up their heads to welcome us and the view down to the valley lay hidden beneath an enchanting blanket of mist. The surrounding hills shone in the early morning light, fields and forests adding colour to the blue canopy that rimmed the mist covered small town. A perfect day to gaze upon the world in all its majesty, and breathe in the pure air while contemplating ones own place in existence. What rubbish! I only saw the dew resting on the grass and knew I would soon be soaking wet from my knees down and the mowers would block with wet grass. Within a few minutes Bob and I would be covered from head to toe in a vegetation soup of shredded grass and weeds as both the petrol strimmer and the mower threw out wet and sticky debris.

The peaceful silence of that delightful morning was suddenly ripped apart as we started both our machines and I headed off with the strimmer to trim around the head stones. Following behind the largest of the mowers, Bob tackled a large area of lawn that was destined to become the next resting place when the present section was full. As foretold, within moments we were both covered in soggy greenery and a film of sweat was blossoming forth upon our brows. It was obvious we would not have the time to complete the task to the high standard we were known for, instead we dashed hither and thither between head stones of all shapes and sizes while trying hard not to smash our equipment on loose stones and fragments of marble or granite that had broken from the stones over the years.

The hurried nature of the work and the physical strain soon began to take its toil upon my mind and it began to wander aimlessly. Eventually I began pondering on the lives of those now resting beneath my feet, though how anyone could rest with the roar of a petrol mower and the stomp of booted feet vibrating down through the ground. I fully expected a spectre to rise from its grave and tell me to shut the heck up.

Names and dates written on the head stones caught my attention briefly at first, but soon the meaning, the emotion and the feelings of loss flooded my thoughts and I began to feel very guilty about disturbing these residents of Boot Hill. Eventually a sensation of being watched crept over me, and I was filled with stories of ghosts and ghoulish apparitions that arose from their slumber during the darkest hours of the night. I have never come to a conclusion regarding the supernatural, most people do not believe in spirits, other than the alcoholic kind, because they have never actually seen a ghost, however I have never seen a million pounds but that does not mean it does not exist. So my mind was open concerning the possibility of a spirit world and therefore it was not too long before my imagination began to see things from the corner of my eyes and the sensation that someone, or something hovered behind me started to run riot in my mind. Names of past souls appeared to leap out at me from the ancient grave stones. Their lives and how they died pressed on my thoughts as I continued to swing the petrol strimmer across the thick wet growth of grass that surrounded their final resting places. Reality faded from my mind and I entered what could only be called a trance like state as my physical actions became automatic while my mind meandered through the dark corridors of the underworld or afterlife.

The work was arduous, the graves had been originally laid in no form of order, headstones, small monuments and flower filled urns made manoeuvring the long shaft of the strimmer difficult and to top it all, it was not long before my stomach began to rumble with hunger. Thus with part of my mind concentrating on the work, another part trying not to concentrate on my stomach, those parts left had little to do but imagine. With my thoughts fixed morbidly upon the deaths of those whose names were carved forever on the stone slabs, my imagination was by now running wild and I was too scared to stop working as I feared what I would hear if I turned off the strimmer.

At that moment a hand landed on my shoulder and a voice carried over the roar of the petrol engine. 'I've finished that lawn. Do you want a break before I get out the small mower?'

Hah, up I went, up to the sky with a terrified scream as I jumped in shock and horror the instant I felt the hand upon my shoulder. A natural bodily function reacted to my fright and I broke wind as I jumped, giving the impression of a jet propelled take off! Upon landing I threw the still running strimmer to one side as my body moved from fart mode into flight mode as I frantically searched for the best route of escape.

'What's up with you?' asked that voice again, 'Give you a fright did I?'

Still in shock I spun around to face my supernatural foe, and found a grinning Bob watching in amusement.

'Give me a fright? I nearly jumped out of my skin! Bloody good job I went to the loo before we started otherwise I'd need a change of trousers now. What the hell were you doing, creeping up on me like that? And while I'm working in a bloody graveyard?' I shouted back at Bob as I attempted to recover my sanity, stop my hands shaking and halt my bladder from emptying into my boots.

'I did call to you several times but you were in a
world of your own and the only way I could get your
attention was to come over and tell you. Your face was
a picture!' laughed Bob as I calmed down.

Still shaking I replied, 'Well you certainly got
my attention. You wait till you have to work amongst
these gravestones, it's a really weird feeling.'

'You thought I was a ghost? Your face is still
white, what the heck were you thinking about?'

'Guess,' I said, 'look around you and take a wild
guess.'

'Ha thought so, but I couldn't resist the chance
to scare the crap outta you. Best laugh I've had for ages!
Gotcha!'

'Yeah, I'll get you for this, I'll have my
revenge,' I grinned as the humour of the situation finally
pierced my frightened brain.

'Can we have a tea break now? Looks like you
need it.' asked Bob.

'Go forth and multiple! But yeah, OK, let's take
a break,' I replied as we both headed towards the van
and our lunch bags.

That was not to be the only fright I received
while working at the cemetery; in fact it was not long

before I needed a sedative in the form of coffee and chocolate before even driving through the cemetery gates. I am glad to say that I was not the only one; Bob himself discovered the secret of flight when a rabbit suddenly leapt from the hedge beside where he was mowing, and ran headlong past the nose of his lawnmower. Bob did not hurt the rabbit with the mower: he was running in the opposite direction! However the biggest fright I received came one misty and gloomy morning. I was strimming between the headstones once more when I noticed a tall gentleman in a large grey raincoat enter the cemetery through the wrought iron gates at the opposite end of the grave yard to where I was working. We often had people attending the cemetery to pay their respects to loved ones or colleagues, laying flowers and bowing their heads in silent prayer. I had even witnessed one chap shouting and gesturing at the side of a grave, as if he insisted on continuing an argument even after death.

I decided it must be his wife's grave.

On this occasion I took little notice of the gentleman entering the cemetery, the weather was gloomy and the grass was wet, so not a day to spend in idle conjecture. I immediately forgot the visitor and continued with the task in hand. Some time later I looked up from the area I was cutting and glanced around in an automatic gesture that I was only barely aware of. I noted that there was no sign of the gentleman so I assumed he had concluded his business and gone on his way. Lowering my head I continued the task of cutting grass around the headstones, ornaments and urns so Bob could follow me with the small mower. I did not usually carry the small lawnmower as it only had a twelve inch cutting radius, however with such narrow space between graves; the little machine came into its own.

Suddenly a tall grey shape materialised right in front of me. Looking up shapely I found myself face to face with the man I had noticed earlier. His long grey coat, grey features and grey hat created a scary vision and it took me some moments to realise he was human! He appeared an elderly gentleman I thought politely, because in truth he looked positively antique. His grey angular face was cragged and lined; his shoulders narrow and hunched though his stance remained firmly up right and rigid. The grey man was tall, very tall; standing well over six foot in height however his frame was excruciatingly thin. My immediate impression was that of a grey spectre hovering slightly above the ground in front of me. Quickly I reached to turn my mower off, thinking if he was indeed human, maybe he wanted to discuss some feature of a particular grave, perhaps some one he loved, or hated, I did not know. As my hand pulled the stop lever, his hands were reaching to undo his long coat. I stared in amazement; surely I was not going to be accosted by a flasher in a cemetery! Taking my eyes briefly off the strange apparition before me, I hurriedly scanned the area to ascertain the whereabouts of Bob in case I needed back up, or a witness. In an instant I saw Bob watching, his posture suggesting he was aware of the grey gentleman undoing his coat right in front of me. However I cannot to this day decide honestly whether Bob was preparing to run to my aid, or collapse laughing.

The grey apparition continued to open his coat, his grey eyes watched me from behind an expressionless grey face. Not one word did he utter or even a sound make, he simply stood there in front of me and slowly opened his long grey coat. After what seemed a millennium but actually consisting of few seconds, the coat came undone and the grey man reached inside. I was still frozen to the spot, wondering and slightly fearing the intentions of the strange figure before me. I noted he was not wearing wellington boots, nor did he appear to be naked and I sighed in relief. Instead of exposing himself to the world and me, he reached into an inner coat pocket and drew out an envelope. Still staring but now in confusion, I could see that the envelope was small, obviously contained a note or letter and had no address or other details marked upon it, only what appeared to be a name. Slowly and silently the grey man lent forward and very gently lifted an ornament from the surface of the grave where we stood. I was standing stock still at the foot of the grave as the grey man bent his long grey trousered legs and carefully placed the envelope under an old cement urn that rested just in front of the weathered headstone. My eyes followed every action the grey man had taken, but now my eyes were drawn to the urn itself and for the first time I noticed that there were several similar envelopes in a piles and secreted beneath the urn. It was on top of this pile that the grey man placed the new envelope before gently replacing the urn. My attention and obviously my curiosity remained on the grave and its little secrets, secrets perhaps or simply letters to a departed soul, I did not know. My attention was only distracted for a matter of seconds before I looked up and realised the grey man had gone, seeming disappearing into thin air, there was no sign of him at all in the quiet cemetery. The only evidence that he had even been there lay undisturbed beneath the small memorial urn upon the grave.

'Oi! You going to finish that bit or just dream all day? Is the strimmer broke again?' called a familiar voice from across the headstones.

'Where did that bloke go? He disappeared quickly didn't he?' I asked Bob while still glancing around the cemetery.

'What bloke?'

'That grey looking bloke who was in front of me a moment ago.'

'Oh him. Dunno mate, I didn't see him leave either but I wasn't paying that much attention. What did he want?' Bob enquired with a distinct lack of interest in his voice.

'I've no idea really. He appeared, left a note or something on this grave and then disappeared again. Even Dynamo, the Impossible Magician couldn't do that!'

'Who?'

'Never mind,' I muttered as I pulled the strimmer in life once more and continued to work my way through the assorted headstones, plaques, beer cans and graves.

The urge to check under the urn and examine the letters flitted through my mind for a split second or so, but I quickly squashed the thought immediately. The appearance of the grey man had un-nerved me slightly and to be honest I was not totally certain that he had actually left the cemetery, and I most certainly did not want him to suddenly reappear while I was rifling through those most private of letters. No way!

I held the maintenance contract for the Boot Hill cemetery for several years and saw many strange things, some sad, some with humour and some that continued to frighten the wind out of me. But on the odd occasion, something different and unexpected happened, not gloomy, not funny, just different, the sort of thing one does not really associate with funerals and cemeteries.

On one particular occasion I had brought Trev along. Trev was standing in for poor Bob who had managed to trip over a match stick and hurt his ankle and Trev offered to step in (pun apologises) and help out. Trev could on occasion be very heavy handed, but as we were just pushing grass cutting machines around all day, I could not see any harm resulting from his assistance. Little did I know!

Arriving at approximately nine o'clock that morning, I say approximately because the very first job I had to undertake that day was to eject Trev from his bed with a large crowbar. Like I said earlier, Trev was still quite a young man. So we duly arrived at the cemetery and Trev jumped from my van in order to open to two iron gates so I could drive in. The gates were old, possibly as old as the cemetery itself, and although still strong, they could be difficult, especially after wet weather and as Noah and his ark had passed the area the week before, I knew we had had wet weather recently. Today the gates offered little concern to Trev, I think they saw him coming and decided to behave. With a loud squeal Trev swung open the gates; it was the gates squealing by the way, not Trev. Once fully open I manoeuvred the Ford van into the cemetery and parked up alongside the left section of grass, making sure I had allowed any other vehicles plenty of room to get past me. I did not think it would be a wise idea to force funeral cars, coffin bearers and weeping relatives to drive or walk over the wet grass because I had caused an obstruction with my van.

Once suitably parked I exited the van in time to see Trev swinging the two heavy gates closed with his usual gusto. It was a condition of our contract that even when working in the cemetery, the gates had to remain closed in order to stop dogs, cows, rabid children and other assorted animals gaining access to the quiet place of rest and doing what animals and children do best. I gave no more thought to the gates as I opened the rear doors of the van and prepared to unload the machinery, Trev turning up a few seconds later to assist. Lifting the first mower out I managed to turn a bright shade of red and howl loudly that my back was hurting. Immediately Trev quietly moved to the front and proceeded to unload all the other machines by himself. Like I had mentioned before, Trev was incredibly strong and unlike many others, he was not afraid to use his muscles in the time honoured physical activity of hard work. As for myself, I counted brains as important as muscles and miraculously my back recovered as soon as Trev lifted the last machine from the van.

Work began as we each moved onto our allotted area of grass, Trev to the long mole infested section on the left. I plodded off right towards the fully occupied forest of headstones with the petrol strimmer balanced loosely in my hand. A rapidly growing hatred for long wet grass; haphazardly placed headstones, random urns, pots and wilting flowers grew within me. Small shrubs, litter, cigarette packets; beer cans, whiskey bottles, used condoms and all forms of detritus native to English graveyards. Almost immediate the twine on the strimmer head broke against a sharp corner of a headstone, making my dismal morning complete as I sat upon a stone slab and began disassembling the strimmer head in order to rethread the twine. Basically it was one of those days when lying in a warm bed at home was more desirable than all the gold in the world.

Finally with the strimmer fixed I set about my work, in the distance I could hear Trev's machine roaring happily as he marched up and down the section of grass lost in his own thoughts. My mind also began to shut down as the monotony of the physical task ahead of me switched my body into automatic mode. Work progressed without any further hold ups, break downs, minor disasters or even the slightest hint of excitement. Wet grass sprayed in a wide radius from the strimmer head, covering me and everything else within its reach in a sticky, smelly broth of grass, weeds, the odd insect or three and – dog poo! I always wore a full face shield when working in the cemetery or caravan parks, not so much to protect me from small debris that the strimmer would fling up, no I wore the face shield to avoid the not so pleasant experience of dog poo in the face. Signs on the gates and placed around the cemetery stated that all dogs should be kept on a lease and any dog mess should be picked up and placed in the appropriate bin. As usual this statement was repeatedly ignored, so a brown splattered face shield was a common event, sadly. It was not long before I had to stop work and head for the tap provided by the local Council for those wishing to water flowers in the urns, tubs or milk bottles situated upon the graves. Once the face shield had been cleaned under the tap and finished with an antiseptic *wet wipe* cloth, I returned to my work and a comatose mind.

Little more that ten minutes after cleaning the mask an unfamiliar sound slowly began to penetrate my wandering brain, in fact it took a couple more minutes for me to identify the sound and drag myself from the depths of an interesting day dream. It was the sound of a car horn. Quickly I looked up from the grass in wonder, why would I hear a car horn blaring in the quiet of a cemetery. Within seconds I noticed a huge black shiny funeral hearse just outside the cemetery gates, its driver gesturing to me in a manner most inappropriate for his profession. Immediately behind the hearse, two more long black limousines headed a line of assorted vehicles, all apparently wishing to gain entry to the cemetery where I now stood in total incomprehension. At the gates stood a well dressed gentleman all in black, he too was alternately gesturing at me while shaking the firmly closed gates . . . Ah ha! The penny dropped! It was a funeral procession that could not complete its task because no one could open the cemetery gates. Who had last closed the gates? Trev!

Sensing the grieving people may desire entry and therefore may possibly not go away and let me finish my job; I switched off my machine with a sigh and headed off towards the gates, collecting Trev along the way. Trev of course had no idea what the problem was and I do not think he had even noticed the black vehicles aligned outside the cemetery gates. Furious stares and muttered curses greeted Trev and me as we neared the obviously stuck tight gates.

'What the hell have you done to these gates?' demanded the gentleman in black, 'I can't open them and in case you can't see, I've a funeral to administer!'

'Not my gates mate,' I replied, slightly offended at his manner, 'but we'll see if we can help though, otherwise you'll have to contact the local council.'

'I haven't got the time to chase some little politician! I have a poor chap awaiting his eternal rest. And several of his friends and family are noticeably upset and could do without this fiasco. Can you help please?'

'We'll have a go, let's have a look and see if we can sort the problem.'

I relented as both Trev and I stepped up to the gates for a closer examination. Immediately I saw the problem. The gates were extremely old, held together by centuries of black paint but little actual metal anymore. With a stern meaningful stare at Trev, which went straight over his head, I pointed to the reason why the gates would not open. The over zealous Trev, with his bulging muscles and heavy-handedness had evidently slammed the gates closed so hard that the feeble metal had buckled and now the locking latch was totally jammed. In fact the gates used to open inwards to allow entry, now they looked like they were in reverse and may only open outwards, if not for the fact that the latch was entirely tangled between both gates.

Both Trev and I began pulling hard at the gates, joined by the gentleman in black who I assumed was a Funeral Director. With many puffs, pants, curses and strains we all heaved and pushed at the gates but to no avail. Soon we were joined by the driver of the hearse and several of the less distraught mourners, including the harassed looking local vicar, all attacking the gates furiously. The scene resembled a sketch from a Benny Hill show, I am sure he would have been proud of it.

Trev and I inside the stuck gates, two funeral persons, one vicar and three mourners, all in black fighting with an ancient pair of wrought iron gates. Still they would not budge. Now I began to get worried, the fact that others could not gain entry to the cemetery was until now, a minor distraction to the otherwise tedious day. But now the realisation hit me that if no one could get in, how was I going to get out. Damn! I increased my efforts and encouraged the others to do likewise, which for some reason offended them. I assume they thought that I considered they were not trying hard enough, they were indeed correct but I considered it too hazardous to my health to point out this opinion at that precise moment.

Red faces and heaving chests finally brought our endeavours to a halt, we realised we had to admit defeat and each of us stepped back and scrutinised the obstinate gates in thought.

'That's it! I'm phoning the council,' declared the Funeral Director, 'they can get out here and sort this out now!'

'Good luck!' I replied as with mutual agreement, Trev and I walked off towards our van for a cup of tea and a snack.

'How hard did you slam those gates?' I asked Trev as soon as we were out of hearing distance from the funeral procession.

'I didn't slam them,' he said, 'I just closed them firmly. Didn't mean to knacker them. What are we going to do?'

'I don't know just yet, let me think about it.'

I sipped my flask tasting tea and considered. Back at the gates, the sound of wails, curses, sobs and threats arose from the gathering of people outside the gates, it seemed all those involved in the funeral had exited their cars and joined the others at the gates. I could hear the Funeral Director pleading with the council clerk in an effort to obtain assistance; I quickly gathered his begging was falling upon suitable deaf civil servant ears. Alternating between sipping my tea and munching a Hobnob biscuit, I came up with an idea but first I needed to ensure there would be no repercussions against me. Leaving the van I once more joined the Funeral Director at the gates.

'Ask him if we can have permission to open the gates ourselves,' I asked the Director who was still pleading his case to the uncaring civil servant on his mobile phone. 'But make sure what ever we do will not result in prosecution.'

The Director looked at me for a moment, obviously fearing what I had planned, before insisting on a promise that none of us would be held accountable for any damage done to the gates during our efforts to open them. The Director was no fool; he put his mobile on speaker phone as the council clerk gave his assurances to ensure multiple witnesses and the vicar to the clerks promise. We could now all hear the clerk's bored response that no action for criminal damage would be taken against any of us, and that he would try to contact a member of the council but was reluctant to disturb any of them. This of course resulted in a furious outburst from all those present, mainly in the form of comments such as;

'Wake the lazy buggers up! What are we paying them for?'

'I'll give them a disturbance! Who the hell do they think they are?'

'The papers will hear of this! Damn councillors, all wind no action!'

'Help us God,' prayed the vicar.

This and other less polite comments rang through the once peaceful valley and the self important council clerk suddenly realised his own job could be as risk here. Bad publicity always requires a 'scapegoat' and in this case it would most likely be him. Instantly his manner changed, he assured us what ever action we took in order to gain entry to, or exit from in my case, would not incur legal action and he would contact members of the council immediately. The Director closed the phone connection with a satisfied twitch off his mouth.

'OK, what have you got in mind then? How are we going to open these damn gates?' he asked me as the phone disappeared into a pocket.

'I'll use my van.' I stated, 'maybe best if you all stood back.' And with that I strode back to my van, closely followed by a very confused Trev.

Back at my van I admitted to myself that I only had a vague idea on what to do, if it did not work then I was just as stuffed as the funeral party. However I manly pushed my doubts to the empty recesses of my mind, and reached for a long thick rope. Handing the rope to Trev, I instructed him to go back to the gates and tie one end of the rope to the gates while I reversed the van nearer. Off went Trev, looking far too happy to have understood what I had said. Sure enough when I backed up the van and got out to inspect his handiwork, I found both gates very securely tied together, tied so securely there was not enough rope left to attach to the

van! Some moments and several grunts later, the rope
was untied, untangled, un-mangled and one end was
attached to the tow hitch of my van, the other end tied to
one of the stuck gates. Realisation of my intentions had
caused the funeral group to take several more steps back
away from the gates, such faith I thought to myself.
Climbing back into the van I began the manoeuvre
which I hoped would open the gates.

It did not. Almost as soon as the rope became
taut as I edged the van forward, the rope snapped with a
crack that I feared would wake the dead. An after
thought concluded that if the dead had awoken, they
could help to open the damn gates. But alas the dead
stayed dead and the gates stayed shut. Next I tried
doubling up the rope, looping it into two lengths before
once more attaching it between the gates and the van. I
discarded the small section that had snapped earlier.
Once again I gently edged the van forward, keeping the
revolutions of the engine high and controlling the van
by riding the clutch.

Snap! Damnit!

Ok I decided, time for plan B – whatever that
was. I had no idea, but Trev did. While I stood just
staring at the broken rope and scratching my head, I
realised the tone of the engine had changed. Trev had

taken the controls and was reversing my van, straight towards the gates! Quickly I leaped out of its path and clamped a hand over my eyes; I did not want to watch my No Claims Bonus disappear into a pair of mangled wrought iron gates. With a slight screech of tyres, my tyres, Trev zoomed towards the gates but slowed just before hitting them. Then with a surprisingly gentle touch of the controls, he eased the tow bar up against the centre of the gates and began to push. Slowly but persistently the van increased the pressure on the gates. Suddenly loud creaks and groans could be heard, and not all of them from me. Then with a mighty screech, the gates parted, stubbornly I admit but part they did, until with a snap they were open. Trev immediately brought my van to a halt before driving slowly forward and away from the gapping gates. Jumping from the now stationary van, Trev rushed over to assist we poor mortals, that being myself, the two funeral personnel and able bodied mourners as we forced the gates fully open. Admittedly the gates now opened out instead of opening inwards as they had done for the last hundred or more years, but at least they were open.

So finally the funeral got under way while Trev and I had another cup of tea and watched the proceedings. Neither of us thought it would be fair to start our machines and continue working while the service was being conducted, it would not seem right after the now infamous fight with the gates at Boot Hill.

Chapter Eight: Digging an Alibi

In the course of our work we travelled to many locations within the county, often places so remote one needed a proficiency in map reading and orienteering to find them. Down narrow county lanes, up farm tracks, through tiny villages, hamlets and Travellers sites. Into major towns, conurbations and business parks we journeyed with nay a care in the world, which was lucky as I have no sense of direction at all. Strangely I hardly ever got lost when searching for a customers location, however in my private life I can forget the route to my local supermarket only two miles away. So it was that on this particular day I accepted a job of work at the other end of the county, an area I was as familiar with as the inside of Buckingham Palace.

The task this time was to dig over and weed a large garden belonging to a property virtually in the middle of nowhere, or so I thought. Actually it turned out to be on the outskirts of a very picturesque hamlet over looking the Atlantic Ocean on the North coast. The property had been newly purchased by my customer and it was his wish that the gardens were cleared and tidied while he worked on making ready the house itself. The work entailed cutting back trees and shrubs, mowing lawns, weeding flower beds and digging over and fertilising the vegetable plots, of which there were several. The customer had hired us for a period of one week in order to complete the tasks in one attack. As the venue was some distance away from my normal circle of work, the week's employment was the only way I would agree to travelling so far, that and the promise of fuel expenses added to the final bill.

Starting an hour earlier in order to make use of the whole day, I picked up Bob and began the long drive to our destination. I knew the general direction of our new customers abode but that was all, so in good faith I headed across the county. This was of course before Satnavs (*satellite navigation*) became available so either one used a map, asked directions or remained lost for hours at a time. I had studied the map of the area, however finding the location of this particular property was more guesswork than intelligence. Plus it was very early in the morning and neither I nor Bob were fully conscious, bleary eyed and constantly yawning, two really good examples of the healthy outdoor life. Carefully we made our way through narrow roads, villages and the odd roadside café for sustaining coffee, all the while hoping we had not forgotten an important tool or piece of equipment because there was no way I was driving home again.

Finally we reached the small hamlet in which our customer's property was located, now all we had to do was find his actual address. After seeking help from many pedestrians, passersby and homeward bound burglars, we at last arrived at the address of the intended victim of our alleged gardening skills. The property was an old building, possibly a couple of hundred years old and constructed from local granite. The garden was quite large, approximately two or three acres and held all the aspects of a country garden. Lawns, flower and rose beds, a small pond, shrubberies and vegetable and fruit plots, in fact it had been so thoroughly laid out that it resembled a Victorian garden and as it turned out, it was. As we headed for the front door we glanced around us, partly in envy but mostly in apprehension at the scale of the task ahead of us. I began to suspect that the allotted time of one week would not be enough. My hand had barely reached to the bell before the door was swung open and we had our first look at the new customer.

Mr Peach was his name but there was nothing peachy about his appearance. Standing tall with hints of grey appearing in his hair, wiry sideburns framed his gaunt cheeks and one would be hard pressed to find any fat upon his scrawny frame. His face appeared tired and pale and his overall appearance suggested a weary man. Horn framed glasses attached to rather over sized ears emphasized piercing blue eyes peered at each of us in turn with a steely glint. No smile brightened his face as he greeted us while pulling on a pair of Wellington boots in preparation for showing us the jobs that required attention. I immediately felt stirrings of dislike but fought them down, it was his custom I wanted not his affection.

With a grunt he lopped off at a quick gait with us trailing behind as he sped through the garden pointing at areas that demanded our attention. His whole manner was that of a preoccupied mind, the garden was viewed as a chore, not an area of pleasure and contemplation. Bob and I followed like two cowed puppies in his wake, mentally taking notes of his instructions and assessing how to attack each task. When we finally came to a halt in the centre of the garden, I discussed details of the job. Bob wandered away from us as he reviewed the work needed. He had reached an area that was completely wild and overgrown. Obviously it had not been touched for years. I could see Bob on the perimeter of my vision as I continued to discuss the work but took little notice. I was trying hard to appear as a professional horticulturalist under Mr Peach's intimidating gaze.

At that moment our conversation was interrupted as suddenly I heard Bob give a shout. Feeling a little annoyed at his ill mannered interruption, I apologised to Mr Peach and turned to see what had caused Bob to cry out, some what desperately I noticed. Pondering his dilemma I glanced quickly around I could see no sign of him. Again I searched and with some minor effort I established his general direction by the sound of his curses rising up from the ground. I turned to Mr Peach in confusion, ready to give my excuses but he was already moving away. Mr Peach appeared to know exactly where Bob was and strode without hesitation to a small overgrown area in an even worse state than the rest of the garden. Mystified I followed Mr Peach, still with Bob's shouts shattering the peace of the garden. I still had no idea where Bob was until Mr Peach came to a halt and stopping beside him, I could see something unusual protruding from the ground. It was Bob's head! Poking up from the ground like a hairy beetroot, though far less polite. He had fallen into a hole hidden from view by the rampant vegetation and had failed to see the pit laying in wait for him like a wild animal trap. But instead of a wild animal, into the trap had fallen a not only wild but an absolutely furious Bob. Reaching down and grasping an arm each, Mr Peach and I dragged Bob from the hole like a giant and very vocal earthworm and dumped him on firmer ground. Laying panting and soiled (*earth type soil, not the other*) on the grass and before Bob give vent to the words that were obviously on his mind, Mr Peach quickly explained that hole had been dug by the previous owner. For what reason the hole was there, he did not know, but it had been forgotten until Bob physically reminded him. Mr Peach brushed his hands clean and apologised in a short gruff manner, it was blatantly obvious that was all Bob was going to get. Our customer was already moving away, intent on finishing the tour as quickly as possible, however he did add that maybe we should add filling the hole as one of our tasks.

Finally the tour was over and Mr Peach marched rapidly back to his house without a further word, leaving us to ascertain which area to assault first.

'Blimey! He's a friendly person ain't he?' muttered Bob as we took our own tour of the garden with Bob still brushing himself with his hands, endeavouring to remove the remaining clinging soil from his person.

'Bit of a cold fish I think. Don't think we'll get a cup of tea here.'

'Nope it doesn't look that way,' I replied, 'but there's a lot to do and I don't fancy spending any more time here than I have to.'

'Wonder why he's so miserable? And why the hurry to get the garden done in one week?' asked Bob and received a shrug of my shoulders in reply as we made our way back to the van to gather the necessary tools.

'Well when he phoned he said it was going to be a surprise for his wife. He has moved into their new home ahead of her as he wants to get the place sorted before she gets here. Least that's what he told me,' I replied.

'Well who was that woman I saw in one of the windows as we drove in then?' enquired Bob.

'Buggered if I know, perhaps he's hired a house keeper. The house is way too big for one bloke to maintain all by himself, it'll take him ages.'

Reaching the parked van I grasped a fork and a shovel from the back. I also picked up my drink bottle. Everyone knows a garden needs a lot of water, but mostly in the form of sweat!

We decided to tackle the vegetable plots first as they resembled a jungle with grass, brambles, Rumex, Dandelions and lost tribes of indigenous locals covered the plots that had obviously not grown any edible vegetables for some time. Luckily the soil was soft and a rich dark brown so digging was not hard and work soon progressed at speed. Around mid morning we received a surprise, Mr Peach appeared with a tray laden with mugs of coffee and plates of biscuits and even chocolate cake. Immediately our initial impression of Mr Peach was replaced with that of approval. Any customer who willingly provided such a spread of refreshments became our favourite and we eagerly tucked into the food and drink. Mr Peach sat down on an upturned bucket and actually began making conversation, it was a definite case of Doctor Jekyll and Mister Hyde as the miserable and abrupt person of two hours ago now chatted amiably with us as we sipped at hot coffee and consumed several slices of delicious chocolate cake.

Mr Peach seemed happy to talk about himself and offered details on why he had moved down to our little corner of the world. It appears that he had owned and run a small accountancy firm but had sold the business and retired early. He had spent much of his life living and working in the city of London and had concluded that he now desired the country life. To us locals, this property where we were sat would be well out of our price range, so as is often the case it fell to a wealthier city person to purchase it. Mr Peach informed us he had moved down four weeks earlier so he could prepare the garden, and his wife would follow soon. Their children were grown and long since left home so he and his wife decided to retire somewhere away from the hustle and bustle of the city.

Our pleasantly chatting customer described his arrival at their new home and his eagerness for a new start. He had a little story to tell us concerning his arrival he said as he wiggled himself comfortable on the bucket. Upon reaching his new home, Mr Peach had discovered a huge bunch of flowers sent by his estate agent in gratitude for the business. Unfortunately when inspecting the accompanying card, Mr Peach was horrified to see that written on the card in big black letters were the words; *Rest in Peace.* In anger Mr Peach immediately telephoned his estate agent and berated him for his choice of words. The estate agent assured Mr Peach that it was a mistake and that he would investigate the card wording and call Mr Peach back with an explanation. Some ten minutes later the estate agent phoned back. The apologetic agent confirmed that the mistake had originated at the florists and would Mr Peach accept the flowers in the good faith they were intended. Mr Peach relented and agreed. The estate agent was relieved and proceeded to inform Mr Peach of the florist's predicament. Somewhere a funeral was taking place with a bunch of flowers on the coffin with a card that read, *Welcome to your new home.*

Our tea break over, Mr Peach left us to continue our work, though we wondered why he had left the garden to the last week before his wife arrived. He had stated that he had moved down nearly four weeks ago and it appeared that he had done absolutely nothing in the garden.

We continued digging, pulling out weeds and driving off stray cattle, goats and other assorted livestock that had inhabited the overgrown vegetable plots. Coffee and chocolate cake swilling round in our stomachs made digging a real effort as now all we wanted to do was sleep. A little later we heard a car roar into life and noticed Mr Peach had driven away. This was quite strange as most customers warned us if they were leaving the property and left any relevant instructions and an estimated time of their return, however we thought no more about it and slogged on.

An hour had passed and we were well into our stride when a quiet voice startled us. Looking up we discovered a beautiful young lady smiling at us from a path near the plots. She was medium height with flowing blond hair that appeared natural, a slim figure dressed in jeans and a T-shirt that clearly displayed her valuable assets. Designer Wellington boots completed the ensemble. The woman looked to be somewhere in her thirties but full of vigour and glowing fitness. Responding to her greeting, we had stopped working and now stood leaning on our gardening implements like a couple of pensioners reminiscing about old times in over an allotment fence. The young lady introduced herself as Janet and appeared to be in a talkative mood. Although we were enjoying the distraction as she talked, I was impatient to get on as we had quite a task ahead of us. I made a move to resume my battle with Mother Nature and her earthen overcoat when Janet broached the reason for her presence. My curiosity won the battle and I once again paused in my work as I stopped to listen.

With a dazzling smile, Janet explained that she had been Mr Peach's secretary for the last five years and had offered to accompany him to his new home and assist him with the move. Janet originated from London and was delighted with the rural life, away from the hectic life of the city. Janet stated that she would have liked to stay longer but Mr Peach had explained that he intended visiting relatives for a couple of weeks and there was no point in her staying here alone. Janet confessed that she and Mr Peach were "quite close" as she put it and she would be very sorry to leave both him and the house and its country location. Today would be her last as she was due to travel back to London tomorrow and she simply did not want to go. Mr Peach was adamant that he wished to see his relatives before burying himself in his new life. Finally with a hint of tears in her eyes, Janet left us to our work and disappeared back into the house.

Bob looked at me with envy clear upon his face. I knew exactly what he was thinking because my thoughts mirrored his.

'Well! The dirty old man!' exclaimed Bob with a grin, 'visiting relatives my arse. He's been up to naughty business while he's been here.'

'Yep, it's no wonder he couldn't find time to sort the garden. I bet he was too exhausted,' I muttered in reply.

'Poor girl, bet she doesn't know that his wife is due in a week and that's the reason Mr Peach wants her gone, nothing to do with him visiting relatives,' Bob said as he violently pushed his shovel into the soil.

'What a stunner though. How the heck did he attract her, and con her into a few dirty weeks in the country, she's certainly younger than him. I wonder why she agreed. If she has been his secretary for five years, she must know he's married.'

'That does explain his mood change from when he showed us round this morning to when he brought out the coffee. Either we interrupted something or he had thoughts of an all together different pursuit. After telling us what he wanted done, he went back to her and sorted out whatever was on his mind.'

I pondered jealously, 'I'll bet within a few weeks he'll be telling his missus he has to return to London to continue some unfinished business.'

With a grunt Bob agreed with me but the subject was then dropped as we continued with the task at hand. We did see the young lady leave early the next day, a taxi arrived and with a tearful embrace, Janet left Mr Peach standing alone on his doorstep. As we watched her departure, Bob sighed, shook his head and muttered,

'Huh! Some people have all the luck. All we get is some customer's randy dog trying to hump our legs!'

We never did get to meet his wife though, as our contract stated we completed the job within the time limit set and left, leaving no trace or clue that we had cleared Mr Peach's garden and not him. His poor wife would be none the wiser. She would never know that it was Bob and me that dug Mr Peach's alibi. We were not asked to return in the future and I sometimes wonder how the threesome were getting on, and if Mr Peach's activities were ever discovered. A discovery that may lead to the marital impeachment of Mr Peach.

Chapter Nine: Arboreal Adventures

As part of our routine garden tasks we were often requested to trim, shorten or remove trees. Large trees that blocked light from windows, restricted views or shaded an area of garden and made plant growth difficult. Fruit trees included the apple which I pruned regularly for several customers, to hedges such as conifers, beech and Escallonia. I carried various hand saws and axes along with a chainsaw and petrol hedge cutter so we were always prepared for such tasks. Mostly the tree surgery chores were completed without mishap mostly that is, but not always. My family rigorously maintained the two First Aid kits carried in the van for occasions such a tree surgery. Although I still have all my limbs, there are a couple of holes where a drill has *slipped* and many scars from numerous cuts over the years. In one case I even managed to stab myself in the right wrist with pointed nosed pliers that were in my pocket at the time. So in my case a First Aid kit was essential and we carried two in the van because Bob could be just as accident prone as I was. I often remember a friend stating happily; "You know you've done a really good job of injuring yourself well when medical professionals flinch at the sight of your wounds."

He could be really cheerful sometimes.

Our health and safety practice was dubious to say the least so when a job came in to remove the top three foot of a fifteen foot leylandii hedge a cry of alarm could be heard from near and far. The hedge divided the two lawns at the Gate House where we maintained the garden and fought mysterious snakes, so we were familiar with the hedge itself and the immediate area surrounding it. Therefore we armed ourselves with the necessary tools, bandages, sticking plasters and hard hats before setting off to borrow a long ladder from a colleague in the landscaping business. Hearing the reason for the ladder, my landscaper colleague burst out laughing before volunteering his service to, as he put it, save us from any harm. Cheek! We declined his offer ungraciously and set off into battle at the Gate House.

Arriving at the property we soon stood before the hedge and considered our task. The hedge was approximately fifteen to eighteen foot tall, some six foot wide and quite solid. The top of the hedge had become untidy with twigs and branches sticking up like antennas on a row of terraced houses. The idea was to trim the top back and level it off into a square edged and flat

surface. No problem. First we manhandled the long
aluminium ladder from the rack on the van, through the
court yard and across the first lawn, trying desperately
to avoid windows; walls, various shrubs, a Weeping
Willow and a stray cat in the process. For those who can
remember the Eric Sykes and Tommy Cooper short film
titled; The Plank, you may have some idea of how Bob
and I appeared whilst carrying the ladder. At last we
were propping the ladder up against the hedge and
attempting to extend the top third section of the three
piece ladder. The top of the ladder finally rested against
the top of the hedge but Bob felt the ladder should be
higher. He wanted the top of the ladder to extend above
the hedge so we would have support while leaning
across the hedge top to cut it. I felt Bob had extended
the ladder far too high but as it was he that was going up
first, I kept my silence. All went well and progress was
made as the first twenty foot length of hedge was
successfully trimmed level and tidy. Bob was slightly
taller than me, only slightly but he never let me forget
that fact, and it was for this reason that Bob had insisted
he was the best person to initiate the hedge trimming. I
did not argue as I get nervous on a thick carpet and
suffer from aerophobia, a fear of heights that is
frequently mistakenly termed vertigo. Vertigo is a

problem caused by the inner ear and has nothing to do with heights. I also suffer from a form of Vertigo, but that is due to the wife, if you get my meaning.

As I have already said, I thought Bob had the ladder extended way too high, the uppermost section of the ladder stood proud of the hedge top by some eight or ten feet. I could not understand Bob's reasoning but hey, it was him up the ladder not me so I decided to let him get on with it. I remained on terra firma and collected the cut branches as they fell to the ground and piled them in a heap in readiness to transport them to the bonfire site at the end of the garden. We did not intend burning the branches for a few weeks as they were too green, too fresh and too wet to ignite. The idea was to allow them to dry out and turn brown before attempting to burn them, green branches produce plumes of smoke but little else, and we certainly did not want the pleasures of stinging eyes and smoke aftershave spoiling our day.

I was bent over yet another stack of branches when I heard a swishing sound, followed immediate by a short scream and a strangled cry for help. Quickly I looked towards the ladder in case it had slipped but saw nothing wrong, until I realised the ladder was not actually on the ground. It was floating in the air horizontal to the top of the hedge. I could hear Bob shouting but there was no sign of him. I rushed around to the opposite side of the hedge and looked up. There was Bob lying prone and hanging on for dear life to the top section of ladder that extended out over the side of the hedge. It resembled a see-saw with Bob clinging on one end tightly while turning the air blue with his insistent shouts for: 'Some bloody help!'

At first the absurdity of the situation was too much for me and I nearly urinated as I laughed so hard at his predicament. A grown man lying flat upon the top of a horizontal aluminium ladder was just too much for me to bear, however Bob's colourful choice of language mixed with threats pulled me to my senses.

Realising that the only way Bob could get himself down was to fall on his head, I searched round for a method of safely retrieving him from his impromptu playground activity. Rushing off with a suggestion that he stayed where he was, I headed for the van and grabbed a broom, a rake and some rope. Running back to the hedge I tied the handles of the rake and broom together to make one long pole. Bob was still shouting and I must say some of the names he called me were embarrassing, some I did not even recognise so I assumed he was still hanging onto the end of the horizontal ladder as it swayed across the top of the hedge.

Once my makeshift pole was ready I poked my head round the hedge and asked; 'Are you ready?'

Without waiting for his reply I returned to the tied pole and reached it up to hook the bottom of the ladder with the rake end of the pole. It took me some time to catch the end of the ladder, I was a hopeless fisherman and it seemed I was having just as little success in catching a long ladder with a garden rake. Bob continued to plead, rant, curse and describe various ways of physical harm if I did not get him the hell down! Finally after many misses I managed to hook the rake onto the ladder and steady it. Slowly I pulled the ladder end down to the ground, watching as Bob began to scuttle down the rungs away from the ladder top as soon as it became less than horizontal. Eventually I got a hand grip on the ladder base and pushed it firmly down against the ground before standing on the bottom rung with all my weight, thus allowing a shaking Bob to fully descend. Once on the ground again, Bob simply sat down and held his head in his hands. I held back my laughter as I was sure he was in no frame of mind for hilarity at this point. Anyway the fun poking and quips would begin soon enough, just as soon as I considered

myself in no danger of attack. To this very day I wished
I had carried a camera, the telling in no way does justice
to the sight of Bob swinging in the breeze on a see-saw
ladder.

After he had a cup of tea and several cigarettes
we examined what had caused the ladder to swing up
and across the hedge. Finally we concluded that Bob
had indeed raised the ladder too high, and in an attempt
to reach some branches sticking up from the opposite
side of the hedge, Bob had climbed further up the ladder
and leaned over. His weight had over come the angle of
balance and had caused the bottom of the ladder to
swing up until his weight counter balanced the
remaining length of the ladder and he was left unable to
move. When Bob was suitably recovered, our very first
task was to lower the ladder to just one foot above the
hedge before I took over at the top trimming the hedge.
The quips, comments and remakes at Bob's expense
followed not long after.

My second battle with a stubborn hedge came
while a young man who liked to be called Spike was
working for me, Bob and Trev were off building a fence
on another job so as he was new to our company of
misfits, it was decided he should accompany me. The

reasoning was simple; I could teach him some aspects of the trade where as the other two would only teach him bad habits. It is well known that new gardeners learn by trowel and error.

Spike was a Goth, meaning he dressed entirely in black and followed the music of that culture. His clothes were black, his boots were black, his hair was jet black and even his finger nails were black. Ear-rings and assorted piercings littered his ears, eyebrows and nose while tattoos festooned his arms. Spike may have appeared threatening if he had not been so thin. Bob had joked that Spiked should stay away from the House of Commons in case someone mistook him for Black Rod. The actual mace I mean, not the Gentleman User of the Black Rod to give the full title.

Despite his appearance, a huge number of my elderly female customs were besotted with Spike, fussing over him like a wayward child. He was constantly being offered food and small gifts mainly in the form of cash tips and was hugged regularly, much to his embarrassment as a hard core Goth. However it must be said that Spike was a genuinely considerate worker, always adding that final touch to ensure the job was completed properly and often spent those extra few minutes of care sweeping away leaves from doorsteps and ensuring his mature fans were safe from harm in their own gardens. His concerns over the feelings of the elderly customers even included him drinking a whole glass of undiluted apple squash, he did not want to appear ungrateful nor point out the fact that the customer did not have a clue when making refreshments. The fact that he had a stomach upset for two days after the drink was a small price to pay for not risking offending the elderly woman who had pressed the drink into his hand. At our next visit however, I quietly pointed out the instructions on the drink bottle label that stated the drink should be diluted with water before consuming to the customer, without Spike being aware of my actions. I also requested that the customer did not mention the offending beverage to protect Spikes feelings. The next drink we were offered was delightful, properly chilled and diluted accordingly. This must have been quite a relief to Spike's bowels.

The job on this particular day involved trimming another leylandii hedge. Not in itself a difficult task as the hedge only stood some six foot tall as it created a green boundary along the front of the property. Not difficult at all, except on the other side of the hedge was a busy main road and the property was located on a blind corner. To add to our concerns, the road was approximately three foot lower than the level of the garden where we stood scratching our heads. A retaining wall provided an edge for the road as there was no pavement in this rural area, so the wall stood at the edge of the road and a formed a platform for the hedge. So from the roadside the hedge was actually about nine foot high and because of the busy road and its kamikaze travellers, we could not even contemplate erecting a ladder. The thought of someone; namely me, standing at the top of the ladder and wielding a pair of hedging shears as some mindless driver hurtled round the blind bend was daunting to say the least. I had a supply of traffic cones in my van, acquired by my son during his college years but a bright orange plastic witch's hat was not a match for half a ton of metal travelling at sixty miles an hour. I decided not to use the cones.

Eventually Spike and I began work trimming the hedge side and top from the safety of the garden while I pondered the problem of how to tackle the other side. The customer came out with a couple of cups of coffee and also queried how we were going to manage the roadside, and if we were properly insured, he was referring to life insurance of course. His strange Scottish grin suggested to me that a car splattered gardener

might just be fun to behold, for him that is. Still I
pondered, even while sipping the coffee while Spike
and the customer compared musical genre, neither had
similar tastes surprisingly, a Scottish dentist and a
young bad clad Goth.

The break over we continued attacking the
hedge with gusto, or bravado, I am not sure which. I
was worried about tackling the road side hedge and I
had begun to suspect that Spike was a tad concerned
also. Suddenly his thin face split in a grin but he said
nothing. I simply assumed he was remembering a
pleasant moment in his black life, but I was wrong.
Finally the dreaded moment arrived, we had finished
cutting the hedge on the garden side and now it was
time to face certain death on the corner of a main road,
road kill gardeners perhaps.

'OK, I've had an idea,' said Spike suddenly as
we gathered our tools and headed out of the garden
towards the road, 'Why don't we use your van?'

'Huh? We can't cut a hedge with a bleddy van!'
I exclaimed.

'Yes we can, we can stand on it to reach the
hedge. The van as a hazard beacon on top of it and its
roof is reasonable strong and flat. And it's easier for the
drivers to see when they come around the bend.'

'Are you serious?' I asked.

'Yeah why not? It'll be fine. Let's give it a go, it's got to be safer than standing on a ladder on that road.'

'Okay. We'll give it a go but who's standing on the van?' I conceded.

'Both of us can. You can jump down and move the van along as we finish one section of the hedge. Come on mate, it'll be fine.'

That statement of; 'It'll be fine' was one I was not happy with. Of all the times I had ended up injured or arrested, the vast majority of those times were preceded by those exact words, "It'll be fine!"

As I could not see any other way of safely achieving our objective I relented and moved the van from the customers drive and, when traffic allowed, placed it alongside the hedge as close as the retaining wall would allow. I had hardly stopped before Spike leaped onto the roof armed with a large pair of hedging shears. How he got there so quickly and easily I have no idea, I do know I had no way of reaching the roof myself and went to retrieve a step ladder. I placed the ladder at the back of the van, away from the oncoming human driven missiles headed directly for us on the road. With apprehension I climbed up the ladder and stepped onto the van roof, throwing my shears before me. I certainly did not want to fall or be knocked off with a pair of sharp shears grasped in my sweaty mitts. Once stood uncertainly upon the roof I joined Spike in clipping violently at the hedge, hoping desperately to complete the job while remaining uninjured or dead. Spike however, appeared to be enjoying himself immensely and was cheerfully waving back at the drivers who gestured aggressively as they swerved to avoid us and the van. It is very strange how a driver will occasionally flatten a pedestrian or scrape a wall with little concern, but will endeavour desperately to avoid hitting another vehicle. So our big white van with its flashing orange light, a laughing and waving Goth and a terrified gardener survived and the hedge was trimmed into a tidy garden boundary once more.

On another occasion when Spike was assisting me in my employment chores it was not a hedge or tree that provided the entertainment, but Spike himself. We had successfully cut down numerous small trees from the property and were now stacking them ready for burning at the far end of the grounds. I say grounds because the area we were clearing was certainly not a garden, more of an overgrown waste land that was once an industrial site. We had been called in to remove all trees, shrubs, weeds, grass, brambles and pygmy tribes so the new owner could park his work vehicles there. Finesse was not an option as we hacked, cut, sawed and chopped down everything in sight. It was a rather pleasant change from the care we had to provide in our normal line of work maintaining gardens of domestic or business properties.

It was coming to the end of the second day at this venue and we were both tired so I decided to start the bonfire. We could rest as we monitored the fire and threw branches on it, as we had cut down the majority of trees the previous day. Eventually a suitable pile stood before us an appropriate distance away from the other piles of wooden debris awaiting the pyre. The area at which we worked was not near any other properties, apart from the stone built shell of a building that the owner intended converting into a garage and store. It had no roof or windows or any form of interior so it was hardly a fire hazard. However we had situated the bonfire some thirty feet away from the shell, just in case. Finally as Spike threw one more bundle of branches onto the pile, I went off to my van to retrieve a can of petrol and some matches with which to ignite the fire. Upon my return, Spike asked if he could do the honours, having never lit a bonfire before. I agreed without thinking and handed over the fuel and the matches before moving away to gather more fuel in the form of branches.

A moment or two later I heard the expected whoosh as the petrol was ignited but it was followed closely by a yell of fright and a thump which I had not expected. Whirling round I saw Spike rise from the ground where he had landed after leaping away from the now blazing fire. Frantically he was slapping his head and pullover while dancing about madly. I rushed over with suspicion in my mind. Sure enough when Spike had finished his poor impression of a Morris Man in May, the proof of what had happened was clearly visible. The front of his once black pullover now had a wide brown singed mark running up its front. Above this was a face no longer bearing any eyebrows and further above this a singed brown fringe sat high upon his once styled black hair. Spike resembled someone who had been run over by a huge roller covered in a dirty brown paint. His appearance now did little to inspire the Goth culture.

'What the hell happened?' I demanded but in truth I already knew.

'The bloody petrol caught fire so fast it caught me before I could get out of the way,' gasped a shocked Spike.

'Yep. It has a habit of doing that,' I grinned.

'Well I didn't know it was going to go up like that. I could have been injured!' stated a now indignant Spike.

'What? Do you mean you've never started a fire with petrol before?'

'No.'

'Well why didn't you say so? I would have showed you how if I'd known,' I responded, now shocked myself.

'I did!' replied Spike, 'I told you I wanted to start the fire coz I've never done it before. I thought it would be easy.'

'It is easy, too easy if you don't get away fast enough. Blimey, I'm sorry, I should have realised,' I admitted sadly.

'That's Okay, I'll know next time.'

'Yeah, when using petrol to start a fire, you throw the match from a safe distance and still run like hell straight away!'

'Cheers mate,' said Spike as the humour of the situation overcame the seriousness of the alternative outcome, 'better late than never.'

With that we both relaxed and added fuel to the fire as required. I did however; keep a close eye on Spike in case he did anything silly, but it was blatantly obvious that Spike was no pyromaniac.

The next adventure concerning the pruning and trimming of trees really turned my world upside down. This time I was working once again with faithful Bob, perhaps not the best choice of employee to have in a difficult situation. He was still seeking revenge for my prank with the pretend snake and my amusement at his amazing see-saw antics at the Gate House.

We were attending a small private garden and the task was to reduce the height of two Lawson's Cypress (*Chamaecyparis lawsoniana*) conifer trees that grew very close together but had become tall and blocked light from the customer's kitchen window. A fairly simple job that entailed one person climbing up between the two trees and with the aid of a chainsaw, remove the top third of growth. It was planned that the main trunk of each tree would be cut but the surrounding upward leaning branches would be left to hide the amputation. As the two trees were so close to each other a ladder would not be needed and I decided, in my wisdom, to simply climb up in the space between. I admit this was a stupid idea but it seemed a good one at the time, climbing with one hand gripping a chainsaw. Nor did I consider using a rope to haul the chainsaw up and down the trees. The two green sentinels only stood about fifteen feet high and I was going to reduce them down to around ten foot tall, no need for either a ladder or a rope, in fact I didn't even bother with a hard hat.

I had known the customer for many years as she lived in the same village as I did, so I was keen to keep the costs down and remove the excess height of the trees as quickly and efficiently as possible. The customer was a locally very well known woman and I knew details and opinions on my work would rippled through the surrounding area like a tide so I had to do the best job I possibly could for as little expense as the job would allow. The customer in question was a large lady, along the lines of a battleship and she definitely knew what she wanted. Providing she got her own way in matters she was a pleasant person, but one would not cross her without suitable life insurance. Her husband was a delightful chap, easy going and likeable, especially by the ladies which annoyed our customer even more. He was by no means an unfaithful husband, though most could not understand why. He was tall with tightly waved dark hair and in very good shape for a man in his fifties. How he stayed with his battleship wife no one understood, but the marriage seemed happy and I never saw them argue nor did I ever see evidence that she attempted to dominant him. They were just a middle aged loving couple happy in each others company; it was the company of others that turned the wife into such a formidable person.

On this day the husband was off at work and our customer was baby sitting her three young grandchildren. The two girls and one boy were reasonably well behaved for under six year olds, but like any child their curiosity abounded, mostly in our direction as we were a fun distraction for the day. Bob and I had a few other chores to do within the garden before we tackled the twin conifers and the children followed our every move with the curse of all parents, inquisitions that included that all time childhood question of: "Why?"

"Why are you doing that? Why is that like that? Why . . ? Why . .? Why . . . ?"

As always one answer led to another question from the curious children and so on it would go on into infinity. We did our best to answer the first hundred questions but finally had to implore their grandmother to save our sanity. The respite from questions lasted a lifetime of ten minutes.

Finally the time came to begin work on the twin trees so the children were herded in doors for safety, and our sanity. While Bob continued with a small job across the garden, I grasped the chainsaw, primed it and began to pull. It had not been used for a few weeks and was always a devil to start after a period of non use. Personally I think it sulked and simply refused to start out of spite. What ever the reason I pulled the start cord again, and again, all the while cursing at the machine under my breath. Finally with a splutter it roared into life and emitted a thick blue cloud of smoke and I gasped my way to the soon to be shortened trees.

As they were so close together it was easy for me to climb up by straddling both trunks. Let me explain that further. I used my right foot to gain a purchase on the right hand tree and used my left on the left tree, simple. Up I went with two legs and one hand, ensuring that the throbbing chainsaw did not amputate either of my legs or even something much more important. Once in position near the top of the twin trees I began to cut, first I attacked the branches, removing them from the main trunk of the right hand tree. The trunk itself followed under my surgical prowess. Once the trunk was cut right through, I carefully removed it by grasping a branch and shoving it away, allowing the it to land along with the amputated branches at the base of the trees for Bob to collect eventually. All was proceeding well, the chainsaw was behaving, which was strange in itself, and the sun was shining, what more could one ask for.

As it happened, a good sense of balance may have helped on that day. I continued to work perched precariously between the two trees when I heard the children invade the garden again, they must have slipped out whilst their grandmother was occupied elsewhere. Fearing they may get hurt if they strayed too close to where I was working, I called for Bob to come a shoo them away. I received no answer, Bob had disappeared out to the van for something and did not hear me. The children came closer. At that point I was struggling to maintain a hold on the chainsaw and swivel my position to allow me a clear view of the children. They say a watched pot never boils, but unwatched children can lead to all sorts of complications. I could not reach to turn off the chainsaw as I needed my free hand to hold on to the branches while I attempted to see where the children were, I could hear their voices quite close but I could not ascertain their location. I soon found out.

Without warning my only free hand lost its grip on a branch and I began to fall. I fell backwards from between the two trees – well my upper body fell. My feet were still firmly trapped in the same position I put them, one jammed between branches in the left hand tree, my right was still stuck in the right side tree. With legs akimbo I fell or rather my body switched from up right to upside down and the chainsaw continued to roar in my grasp. Frantically I shouted for Bob, I had found where the children were playing. They were right below me! Within seconds I was dangling up side down with each leg stuck firmly in opposite trees, a menacing chainsaw grasped tightly in my right hand while my left searched desperately for a hand hold on a branch. The chainsaw dangled just feet above where the children sat staring up at me in wonder, innocently unaware of the danger. All they saw was a strange man hanging upside down with his legs spread wide between two trees. A sight to behold!

Finally my terrified shouts attracted the attention of Bob. Without a word he rushed over and picked up all three children in one sweep of his arms and rushed them away from the ripping teeth of the chainsaw. Giggles filled the air as the children enjoyed the game with their new playmate Bob, and the highly amusing man upside down in the trees. Bob placed the children in the care of their grandmother who had reappeared at the back door to discover the source of the racket. Bob firmly instructed the grandmother to keep the children out of the garden. Then Bob ran back to me, carefully reaching up, he took the chainsaw from my sweaty grasp and switched it off. Then he stood back, looked at me in my predicament and burst out laughing. He laughed so hard I thought he would wet himself, or at least I hoped he would wet himself I concluded bitterly.

'Well come one then, give me a hand,' I shouted, 'both my feet are trapped and, in case you haven't noticed, I'M UPSIDE DOWN!'

'Ah, I wondered why your face was so red, its blood rushing to your head and filling all that empty space,' he gasped in between guffaws of laughter.

'Stop sodding about and get me down from here!'

'OK, hang on – hahahaha,' laughed Bob at his little joke, 'don't go away.'

'Alright, alright, enough of the jokes. Get me down before the customer calls the Fire Brigade.'

'Right ho, I'll just go and get the big loppers. Think I need to remove a branch or three to get you down.'

Bob headed off to the van while wiping tears of laughter from his eyes.

'Are you alright young man?' said a voice below me.

It was our customer who had decided to check that there was nothing unsavoury taking place in her garden. She was ever a trusting soul.

'Yes I'm fine,' I replied in the calmest tone I could muster, 'my colleague has gone to get a tool to free my feet. Once that's done we'll continue shortening these trees for you.'

'That's nice. Are you sure you don't want me to get help? Is your man really able to get you safely down?' she asked.

'Well I don't know about safely, knowing him but at least I'll get down. I hope.'

'Alright but please shout if you need further assistance, in the mean time I will put the kettle on, I'm sure you'll be grateful for a cup of tea after this,' and with this parting offer the customer headed back indoors the make tea and assess the damage done to her home in the time she had left the children alone.

Bob reappeared finally and stood below me as he pondered the best or funniest way possible to free me. After some too long moments I shouted at him to get a move on. Just for spite he waited several more moments while pretending to consider how to begin. Reaching up with the large loppers, Bob attacked the first branch that he considered would help free me. Of course it did not; in fact he had cut a branch that was no where near the ones trapping my feet.

'What the hell are you doing?' I demanded.

'Just making sure you'll fall right,' Bob answered.

'Right on my head?' I queried.

'Yep!' said Bob.

Snap! Bob had finally cut through one of the branches that held my foot. I was still not able to free it until he cut another that was pressing firmly down across the bridge of my foot. At last my right foot was free.

'That'll do,' I said as Bob moved to the other tree and my left foot. 'I can get myself free now – I think.'

With that I managed to lower my right foot onto another branch with enough of a foothold to enable me to reach up and gradually climb back up the tree until I was finally able to free my left foot.

At last I was free of my impromptu imprisonment and I jumped to the ground with a grunt. As soon as my feet hit the ground something landed on my head. A *splat* sound was heard moments before a horrendous smell appeared. Reaching up to my head I discovered what seemed to be a bundle of twigs. Grasping it I pulled it off my head and lowered it for inspection. I held in my hand a crown of twigs, a discarded birds nest had been dislodged and had fallen from one of the trees I had recently vacated. The smell came from two very rotten eggs that had rested in the nest for sometime before I disturbed them. Now the odorous contents of the eggs dribbled down my face. First I had been hung upside down, now I smelt like a stagnant sewer. What a day!

Wiping pungent goo from my eyes I noticed Bob had moved away some distance, away from the smell but still near enough for me to see his shoulders shaking with laughter at my predicament.

'Serves you right!' he called to me while still sniggering, 'That's payback for the pretend snake prank and laughing at me stuck on the hedge at the Gate House! Wish I'd had a camera.'

I did not say a word; I was just relieved to have escaped a life as a tree decoration. And it was not even Christmas! I did need a wash though. Desperately!

Over the years I had many more misadventures with tree, shrubs and assorted arboreal life forms but none that scared me so much as this one. In all the other tree misdemeanours no one was in any real danger and certainly no children. I was thankfully that this latest escapade had only resulted in my embarrassment and no one was injured. Bob however decided it was a moment in time to cherish, a story that he never failed to relate over a pint or even a mug of tea, he told anyone and everyone who would listen for months afterwards. But it was not long before I had my revenge.

Chapter Ten: Retirement boredom.

As in any business that deals with the general public, we met many odd and sometimes downright strange customers in our meanderings as mobile gardeners. Or horticultural assassins, depending on how one viewed our accomplishments. There are many reasons why a home owner or business proprietor would choose to have someone tend their gardens and grounds. Mostly it is obviously to keep the property tidy and neat, but on occasion the reasons can be some what diverse. On one particular occasion we were called to a property in a quaint little fishing village that had evolved into a modern *honey pot* better known as a tourist attraction.

People came from all over the country, flocking in droves to witness the history of our native fishing industry. No doubt they were all expecting to find fishermen gathered on the quay, fixing their nets and smoking clay pipes. Other expectations may have included women gutting and drying fish on the beach and young urchins in flat caps and short trousers running cheerfully through the narrow lanes between the ancient hovels and homes. Sadly they found another world, a world all tourists are familiar with. Gift shops littered the village like confetti. Shops designed to reflect the popular historical misconception of such seaside villages, while attempting to sell small fishing nets attached to bamboo poles. All kinds of beach apparel, air filled toys, plastic footballs and toy crabs jutted out onto the narrow pavements, carefully positioned to block the passage of any passerby and entrap them in the shop premises.

Food venues vied for business with advertising boards placed outside the properties displaying a range of goods in white chalk writing, often illegible. Local food was on offer in every available position of the village, tourists gather in queues to pay the exuberant prices that are inevitably hiked up during the holiday season.

Motor vehicles engage combat with delivery vans, lost tourists and angry locals merely trying to get on with their lives, their work or their pastimes in another village or nearby town. Invariably all car parks and roads become full to capacity and neither a local inhabitant or tourist could move more than two hundred yards each hour. And I had to drive my van through this mass of confusion, complexity and frustration each time I was required to attend the property of Mr. Jones, in fact on a weekly basis. Oh joy!

Along with the blockage of steel came the mass of humanity, the variety of colours, shapes and sizes adding to the obstacles and hazards that faced the weary traveller as they attempted to make headway through the ancient narrow lanes and streets comically termed roads by those in authority – and ignorance. First into combat was the family unit, mother, father and a horde of children. The parents tired and irritable and the children hyperactive as the sights, sounds and smells of the village assaulted their eager minds as they dashed from shop to shop and caring not a jot for the local history. Parents and relatives of older children, many with children of their own sucked on ice creams or gulped down chips before the squadrons of sea gulls ripped them from their greasy fingers.

Fathers dressed in colourful and often stained vests, sure in themselves that the appearance they portrayed was that of a muscular and virile male. They had no idea that their fat hairy bare arms with antique faded black tattoos and their large bellies, ridiculous flowery shorts and soiled floppy hat perched upon a balding head gave off a totally different impression to all in the vicinity. Wives and mothers also portrayed a personal image that obviously did not resemble the picture they held of themselves in their own minds. Tee shirts and shorts at least one size too small, cheap plastic sun glasses and flimsy foot wear, usually of the *flip-flop* variety adorned these Amazons of modern femininity that deemed to grace our small villages with their presence. Inevitably their chubby hands alternated between grasping at unruly children and stuffing ice cream, sweets and pastries into their plump faces. Bedecked in cheap jewellery with huge hand bags or back packs slung carelessly over ample shoulders that rain an assault on anyone attempting to get past on the miniscule pavements. Holidaying female teenagers almost dressed as they prowl the narrow streets in search of that holiday romance, a fact the local male youngsters were well aware of and make good use of their time. Male teenagers suffering the embarrassment of a holiday with the family stomp sullenly along with heads bowed in defeat, hands stuffed into pockets and ear phones jammed tightly into their ears in a futile defence against the tide of embarrassing humanity surrounding them. The more fashion conscious *lad about town* sweats profusely in his black hoodie while his over sized jeans hand low across his buttocks. Other youngsters and all adults look on in amazement at the chosen attire, the majority of locals and visitors choosing light T-shirts and shorts more appropriate to the summer climate. With rain coats and umbrellas tucked under arms or stashed in bags in readiness for the inevitable British summer monsoon of course, just in case.

Through this mêlée marches the determined tourist, usually a tall gaunt male of mature years. This individual camouflages his presence with a light brown checked shirt over brown corduroy trousers, open leather sandals and thick grey socks. A beaten old wide brimmed hat sits upon his grey head and a worn rucksack hangs limply from his thin shoulders. With huge strides this refugee from a safari moves rapidly through the throngs of humanity, talking to no one and staring straight ahead at all times. Courteous to those women in his pathway, sullen and superior to any male smaller than himself, the determined tourist continues on his way to see every thing possible and absolutely steadfast in his desire to enjoy his holiday.

Finally those narrow pavements that line cobbled streets meet the formidable attack from an overwhelming enemy, the pensioner coach trippers. These groups of elderly ladies, occasionally trailed by timid elderly males, stomp through the village and refuse to make way for anyone. Women with prams or pushchairs, even people struggling on crutches have no defence. Wheelchair users, families and especially any poor local attempting to pursue his/her business are forced aside as one would brush aside a fly. Nothing can stand in their way, except of course an intimidating gang of more pensioners who every one knows; actually own the pavement. When the immovable object known as holidaying pensioners meet the irresistible force acknowledged as the elderly day trippers, normal people flee and head for the hills.

The seaside fishing village lay in a deep valley with the surrounding hills covered in the homes of the wealthy, the retired and those seeking escape from urban living far from the hustle and bustle of city life. It was upon such a hill that Mr Jones enjoyed the panoramic harbour views, safe in his Englishman's castle, a three bed roomed bungalow that mirrored the other properties around him. Spacious but not over large gardens provided a retirement hobby and an up sloping drive led up to a detached garage on one side of the bungalow. A high Escallonia hedge marked the boundary of his property and provided a defence against any efforts at friendship that may emanate from a neighbour. It is strange that the poor and the really wealthy are happy to be garrulous with their neighbours.

But those who consider themselves in the middle, not poor nor very wealthy, the middle classes as they are often referred to, insist on solitude and shun any friendly advances from neighbours or fellow residents. Mr Jones, though a likable gentleman was no different and admitted he did not know the majority of dwellers that shared his section of the hill side. This was a shame and an obvious over sight on behalf of Mr Jones.

Upon arriving the property, the very first thing that Bob and I noticed was the state of the garden, it was immaculate! Trimmed lawns, well stocked clean flower beds, weed free paths and healthy shrubs painted a biscuit tin image in its perfection. I glanced at Bob as we climbed from the van and found him looking back at me.

'What the heck are we doing here? There's nothing to do.'

Making sure no one was within hearing I replied, 'I have no idea. Surely the customer doesn't need a gardener. But we'll soon find out because here he comes.'

Mr Jones was a tall elderly man with small spectacles, thin white hair and a slight stoop. Dressed in the habitual attire of brown corduroy trousers, tan shirt and fawn sleeveless jumper, Mr Jones looked like any other gentlemen of his age and financial bracket. The only thing that set him apart was the wide and warm smile on his face. Out shot his hand in greeting as he enthusiastically welcomed us to his retirement abode.

'Welcome, welcome. It's delightful to see you. (*pause*) I assume you've come to maintain my grounds, we spoke on the phone?'

'Morning Mr Jones, yes that's right,' I responded while grasping his hand in a firm handshake before he moved on to welcome Bob in the same fashion.

Introductions completed, Mr Jones showed us around his garden and gave us instructions on what we were to do. Basically at the rear of his property the garden was divided into two lawns with a meandering path between them, with flower and shrub beds surrounding the whole scene. Our instructions on that day were to reposition the path. Mr Jones had spent some time marking off the area where the new path was to go so there was little prospect of us messing things up by misplacing it. The path itself consisted of white gravel so our first job was to scoop this up into the sacks provided by Mr Jones. He was an extremely organised individual.

We spent the rest of that day cutting away sections of the existing left hand lawn, moving and placing them in the new locations as dictated by our customer's design. Personally I could see little difference in the end result. The path curved slightly more and was now situated a couple of foot to the left of its original position. The path now snaked in numerous directions between the two lawns and around flower beds. I came to the conclusion that Mr Jones had secretly designed an exercise route where he could enjoy a daily walk. It certainly took longer to navigate the simple garden path than really necessary. However Mr Jones appeared delighted and booked us there and then to return on a weekly basis. Neither Bob nor I could understand why our services would be necessary every week, Mr Jones obviously tended the lawns and beds himself, but who was I to question. I was convinced that after a couple of weeks Mr Jones would realise he did not really need us to attend so often, but as he was a paying customer I was happy to continue. Even the arduous task of forcing my way through the throngs of holidaymakers and locals all vying for passage through the narrow streets did not subdue my eagerness for a paying customer.

The following week Mr Jones had deliberately left all the lawns uncut, thus ensuring there was work for us. It only took an hour but he still appeared pleased. Each week we arrived at the property of Mr Jones and completed what ever task he set. We moved both of the rear lawns numerous times, dug up and replanted shrubs, cleaned his greenhouse regularly and even scrubbed down the few slate steps that lead from the drive up to his front door. We continued to mow the lawns, whether they needed it or not and no weed dared show its face without being rapidly ripped from the ground. Mr Jones garden virtually sparked it was so clean and tidy.

Each visit was always interspersed with long tea breaks when Mrs Jones would appear with a laden tray, shadowed of course by Mr Jones. Mrs Jones was a quiet woman, not surprising really as Mr Jones seldom allowed her to get a word in. She was as short as Mr Jones was tall, grey hair pulled tightly back in a bun and the constant uniform appeared to be a pleated skirt, white blouse and a cardigan of either grey or tan. There was never a bright colour to disturb her sombre appearance. However Mrs Jones was very pleasant and had a serious sense of humour, leaving us creased in merriment with her anecdotes and witticisms, most at the expense of her husband.

It was during one of these tea breaks when we discovered why we had been instructed to attend the immaculate garden of Mr Jones each and every week. On that particular day Mr Jones was confined to his bed with a chest infection. Mrs Jones took this opportunity to explain our regular and often pointless visits. She explained that in his working career, Mr Jones worked in a firm that employed hundreds of people and his position within that firm held a high level of responsibility. He had loved his job and was deeply saddened when the time arrived for him to retire. Suddenly he found himself at home all day with only his long suffering wife for company, and he certainly did not dare order her about as he had with his work subordinates. It was through boredom that we were hired, a chance for company once a week and of course, someone to order about. Mrs Jones explained her husband spent hours examining the garden in search of jobs we could do in order to justify our attendance. She admitted she was happy for us to continue to maintain the garden but as Mr Jones was absent, she took the opportunity to request that we reduce our visits to once a fortnight. I agreed, though sad to lose the hours work each fortnight but delighted not to be forced to plough through the tide of humanity so regularly.

So the reason for our attendance at the property of Mr Jones and his fanatically manicured garden turned out to be – boredom. Mr Jones was bored. At that point I remembered his comments on not knowing any of his neighbours and so I suggested to Mrs Jones that her husband initiated a neighbourhood watch or some other form of neighbourly activity. I stated that if he had friends around him, possibly he would be able to overcome his feelings of loneliness and boredom. I had unwittingly shot myself in my foot! Within just a few months Mr Jones had totally organised all the residence of his road. He had even instigated a gardening party consisting of a group of retired gentleman who, like himself were bored with retirement. Mrs Jones had followed my suggestion but unfortunately some months after the organisation of his neighbours, Mr Jones cancelled our services. He now had plenty to occupy his time and this included having the residents gardening group attend his property. He never called again.

Chapter Eleven: A Puzzle.

On occasion it was the task required that caused some confusion and not just the odd antics of a customer. A call had come in for us to lay a patio for a customer within my own village. Of course I was delighted, patios were a pleasant change from mowing lawns, weeding flower beds and falling from hedges and trees. I was also pleased that the location of this job was near to my home, thus reducing travelling time and allowing me to pop home for lunch if so desired. Bob was with me again and he too looked forward to a change in our mundane routine. We should have known better.

The customer was a Mr Lowe who owned a large house right in the centre of our small village. The village was a typical rural community with one successful and popular school, a butchers shop, corner shop, a small garage and a beauty parlour. I never understood the location of a beauty parlour in the village, from what I could see of my fellow residents, the beauty parlour was failing, and we were past help. Our village did have a claim to fame, not much of one but still something to require an annual street fair and get ourselves on the tourist map. Unfortunately it appears the tourists in question could not read and very few ever entered our village intentionally. It was not due to the inhabitants, we were a happy and welcoming village, it was the fact that we were on a route to a more famous town a few miles away and so everyone simply drove straight through and rarely stopped.

Our small claim to fame originated from the passing through of a famous author in the past. The author in question is known and loved world wide so in an effort to boost trade and raise our position in the tourist's guide, we set about declaring our history with the said author. In truth the village's claim to fame was actually the brief visit by the very famous author who once stopped in the village to use the public convenience and purchase a newspaper.

Mr Lowe's house was quite large, at least four bedrooms and dating from the nineteenth century I think. Anyway it was a grand house with a small garden to the front, a drive running down one side of the house and a good sized lawn area at the rear. Mr Lowe required us to lay a patio behind the garage and place a rotary washing in the centre. Simple I hear you cry. No I say in reply. There was nothing simple about Mr Lowes planned design for the patio. Firstly the area to cover measured approximately fifteen feet by fifteen feet, not too big so there was no need to worry on that aspect. It was his design that was to cause the problem. Mr Lowe wanted three different sizes of patio slab. But all laid in no repeated pattern! So if a line of two foot square slabs were laid in one line, we could not repeat this, it was a form of crazy paving without the crazy. On top of this there were two colours of slab, half grey and the other half fawn and there were three hundred and sixty slabs in total. Two foot square slabs, eighteen inch square slabs and twelve inch square slabs, and no pattern. At the reading, this problem may not appear too difficult, but in fact it would have been an excellent pre-entry test for Mensa. It took Mr Lowe, his wife, their two children, their dog, me and even Bob about three days scratching our collective heads and sweating over the mathematics to finally work out how to begin this momentous task.

Bob and I started with a line of two foot square slabs just to get it out the way. The lines of the eighteen inch square slabs and the twelve inch square ones. Each of these lines were placed some distance apart from the other and laid in different directions to ensure even this did not represent a pattern. Then began the fun and dear old Mr Lowe chucked yet another spanner in the works by stating he wanted two of the patio edges shaped in an octagonal manner. The other two were not included in the equations as one butted up against the rear of the garage and the other one ran parallel to the stone wall that provided a border to his property. I decided we would worry about this additional aspect when the majority of the patio was completed; I had a headache by now anyway. Our final plan was to temporarily lay an assortment of slabs down, similar to placing pieces of a jigsaw puzzle on the board before actually fitting them into position. I was never any good at puzzles so this whole episode did little for my state of health. Cross eyed and thick headed, my poor little brain worked over time and did not enjoy it at all. However I soldiered on, braving the intellectual challenge that faced me. Bob too began to show signs of strain, our usual level of thought consisted of which way to push the mower or a choice between a fork and a spade.

After several days most of the patio was in place and Bob and I were mental wrecks. We had arrived at the proposed edge of the patio and were now busy contemplating how to achieve the octagonal outer rim when Mr Lowe had his one and only good idea. We had at last finished the patio but were still fretting over how to achieve the desired shape. We decided that a cup of tea may add power to our brain cells and we paused from the mental exertion of that strange habit commonly known as thinking. Suddenly Mr Lowe leap up and rushed off, leaving us standing with steaming mugs of tea in our hands. Although we were surprised at his actions, we managed not to spill a drop of the brown nectar as we watched Mr Lowe disappear off in his car. Bewildered and confused, Bob and I took the only action we could; we sat and finished our drink and awaited the conclusion of our customer's energetic vanishing act. He returned about thirty minutes later and leapt from his vehicle with a happy but slightly maniacal grin and an industrial angle grinder.

The solution Mr Lowe had arrived at was to simply cut the paved edges of the patio to his desired shape. Bob and I allowed him to get on with it, happy to relinquish the responsibility and rest our tired and over worked brains. In order to achieve the shape required desired by a truly hazardous customer, Bob and I laid slabs where necessary and removed those not wanted. All this was done quite hurriedly as Mr Lowe was following us with the huge grinder and its whirling stone cutting blade. Our enthusiastic customer wielded the grinder like a knight in armour wielding his broadsword. An intense expression lined the face of Mr Lowe, made all the more frightening by the sweat streaks running down his face and leaving tracks through the layer dust that had accumulated on his features. My impression of him at that time resembled a raging Native American Indian swinging a tomahawk at the invading white men in silly hats. Furious hours followed with Bob and me running, lifting and laying different sized slabs round the patio edge while appearing to be chased by a mechanised version of *The Shining*.

When the dust cloud settled and the grinder had fallen silent at the end of the day, we all stood and admired one of the strangest patio's we had ever laid. Mr Lowe was delighted; Mrs Lowe chose to reserve her opinion until we were gone. The children could not care less and the dog chose to urinate on as many parts of the patio possible before being told to go away. Wearily and with aching heads, Bob and I left the completed job and looked for something easier, building a spaceship for example.

Chapter Twelve: Hello sailor.

Our escapade with the patio now a disturbing memory of the past, the business of Green Fingers continued on its way. Bob, Trev and Spike all played a huge part in building the business and all remained with me for some time. Although I only required one employee on a regular basis I did often need all three reprobates together on occasions when my order book became too full. It was during one of these busy periods when Bob and Trev were both with me as we attempted to complete all the jobs booked for that week. I had left Spike at another property to complete some work there. Spike was intelligent and sensible enough to undertake jobs on his own, Bob and Trev often needed guidance, quite a lot of guidance actually. So it was with Bob and Trev that I first encountered Mrs Hogh.

Mrs Hogh and her husband were an elderly couple as were the majority of my customers. Both were in their seventies and both were hard of hearing which made things a tad difficult. I later discovered that Mr Hogh did not have any physical hearing problems, his hearing had simply become selective over the years and upon meeting Mrs Hogh, I could both understand and sympathise. Mrs Hogh chatted incessantly, hardly pausing for breath as she appeared to vocalise each and every thought that entered her head. Apart from that little oddity Mr and Mrs Hogh were a lovely couple and we were made most welcome.

The Hogh residence was a terraced cottage of about two hundred years old, a piece of history with modern double glazing and a shiny new conservatory running along the rear of the building. A small patio separated the house and conservatory from the garden, with the obligatory plastic garden furniture and plastic flower tubs littering its surface. The garden itself was of a reasonable size, the width of the house and approximately seventy yards long, slopping gently down to a block wall where a garden gate lead to another small area that had originally been considered for the purpose of parking their car. Unfortunately this area backed on to the rear of another house situated beside the main road, and the only other access into part of the garden was through a narrow alley that led from the road to the Hogh's garden. A problem had arisen as soon as the Hogh's attempted to drive their car through this alley and onto the space they desired as a car park. The alley itself turned at a sharp right angle from the road and made the entry of a motor vehicle extremely difficult. Thus after one single attempt, Mr Hogh gave up and continued parking his car on a very small plot at the front of his cottage. Access to this space was almost as difficult as the now defunct area at the bottom of the garden. At the front of the Hogh's property a narrow and ancient lane offered access to all the properties in the row of terraced cottages. The lane was so narrow that turning was impossible and one had to drive in but reverse the whole length in order to get out again. I found this out on my first visit and I must say a Ford transit van was almost too wide for the lane. I only managed to get out by folding in my wing mirrors which made reversing all the more difficult.

Following the initial and unsuccessful parking trial, the small area at the very bottom of the Hogh's garden had remained untouched, or so we thought. A minor memory loss on behalf of Mr and Mrs Hogh led to a surprising find some time later. Following the introductions, Mrs Hogh gave Bob and me our instructions for her garden. There was a lot to do and we had been booked for three days. Although not large, the garden had hedges, lawns, flower beds and shrubberies that all required attention. Due to their age, the Hogh's were now finding their garden too strenuous to tackle themselves. I could understand this as I peered at the profusion of growth before me.

Utilising the personal abilities of my two colleagues, I first set Trev to trimming a Box (*Buxus*) hedge that ran most of the way down one side of the garden. These hedges can be quite tough to trim but difficult to harm or damage so Trev was ideal for the job. A Beech hedge (*Fagus sylvatica*) formed a boundary on the opposite side of the garden and Bob was lumbered with that chore. Beech required a little more care and attention than the virtually indestructible Box hedge but I was sure Bob could not damage it or himself, however I did keep a watchful eye on him just in case. I myself set about trimming and pruning some of the more delicate shrubs such as Jasmine (*Jasminum*) and Azalea (*Rhododendron*), plus the many other form of shrub that scattered across the garden. Soon there were piles of hedge and shrub amputations that needed to be cleared and the advice of either Mr or Mrs Hogh was required. Of course it was Mrs Hogh that sped from her back door, already gasping in air in anticipation of the endless flow of words set to issue forth from her mouth.

'You can stack all the branches in that space on the other side of the gate,' she instructed while pointing down the garden, 'we often have bonfires there so that can be a job for later.'

'Okay thank you Mrs Hogh. Trev, can you start carrying all the branches down there, through that gate at the bottom. Just pile it all up ready to burn. Bob and I will clear our rubbish and bring it down as well.'

With everyone busy I began raking together my own litter from the shrubs and my mind was already giving thought to our next tasks within the garden.

'Oi!'

I looked up as I recognised Trev's linguistic skills and turned to look to where he stood in obvious confusion by the open gate at the bottom of the garden.

'What?' I shouted as I dropped the rake and began moving towards him.

'Can't get any more in here,' he replied.

I could not understand what he meant, until I reached the gate and looked over into the area on the other side of the wall. With a shock I saw that the area was totally covered in brambles. It was obvious no one had been down here for years. There had certainly been no bonfires here lately. I wondered which era Mrs Hogh was remembering when she stated that they used this area for bonfires. I also rebuked myself for not noticing just how overgrown this space was. I had walked around the garden when I came to give an estimate a couple of weeks ago but I had most likely taken the word of our customers regarding the condition of the unused parking space. Now looking across the area I could clearly see it was completely overgrown by brambles to a height of about four foot. Several new tree saplings were growing amidst the thorns and I swear I saw a group of garden gnomes frolicking under the foliage. With a sigh I realised we would be on this job a lot longer than I originally thought. Wishing for some cotton wool to stick in my ears, I set off to find Mrs Hogh and discover her wishes for this area. If we were required to clear it I would have to amend my bill and allow for at least one more day, possibly two.

I was lucky, Mrs Hogh was having her morning coffee and even she could not drink coffee, eat a biscuit and deafen me at the same time. Therefore her response was short, she did want that area cleared and she would be happy to pay for the extra time. Quickly I thanked her and returned to the safety of the garden where I instructed Bob and Trev on our additional orders. Bob looked at me in dismay, he had gone down the garden to look for himself and his experience told him what to expect. It was not that long ago when we had fought to rediscover Mr Music's lawn from the grasp of brambles. Trev of course could not care less, at least here he would not have to worry about breaking or killing anything so he could let lose his muscles. As for myself I was pondering how I would complete the outstanding work on my other job locations. I concluded I would bring Spike in on this task the next day in order to accomplish the clearing as quickly as possible. Four men should be able to clear a patch of brambles in one day, hopefully?

Thinking too much had now given me a headache so I decided we would concentrate on tidying the garden itself that day, the brambles could wait until reinforcements arrived. I gave instructions to Bob and Trev and we set about the tasks we had originally planned. Trev went off to get one of the mowers from my van while Bob and I worked to weed and clean the flower beds. The piles of branches had been careful thrown on top of the brambles as we simply did not have any other room for them. For the rest of the day we worked hard, barely stopping for breaks in our haste to do as much as possible before entering into a bramble battle. Mr and Mrs Hogh were not forthcoming with refreshments as many of our other customers did, so we restricted ourselves to our own sandwiches and flasks of tea. Finally at the end of the day we had accomplished a great deal and the elderly couple appeared to be pleased.

Bundling all the tools and equipment back into the van, we set off home for a well earned rest.

The next day saw Bob, Trev and Spike vacating the van outside the property of the Hogh's armed to the teeth with all forms of cutting implements. The small gate left little room for four of us to attack the brambles so I sent Trev and Spike out to gain entry from the alley entrance on the main road. Bob and I would hack our way in from the front while Trev and Spike fought towards us from the rear. We had only been cutting for a few moments when I heard a loud clang. This was closely followed by some expletives from Trev. Trev of course was entirely at home thrashing his way through brambles and consequently had moved far deeper into the thorns then the rest of us. Although I could see Trev over the brambles, none of us could see what he had hit. As Bob and I could not physically reach him, I asked Spike to discover what Trev had hit and if he had broken something valuable. As I mentioned earlier, Spike despite his appearance, was intelligent enough to be trusted in his examination of the problem. In moments he had made his way over to where Trev stood and danced round the road block called Trev.

'It looks like some form of trailer, I can see a metal frame and two road wheels underneath this stuff,' he said while gesturing at the entanglement of thorns.

'Okay. Take it a bit easier until we discover what it is for sure. Trev, take care not to bust any of the tools on that metal work,' I directed.

For the next fifteen minutes we all worked towards the mystery item hidden by nature, I began to feel like Prince Charming battling through the overgrowth to reach Sleeping Beauty. Like I have said before, the mind wanders when one is having such fun as hacking brambles. Finally it became clear that the obstruction was indeed a trailer, a twin wheeled boat trailer by its appearance. How the heck someone managed to get it in there defied logic, it was obviously over twenty five foot long and about seven foot wide. Twin rails attached to the trailer frame suggested the capacity to haul a large boat but at the time in my illustrious life, I knew very little about boats so my conclusions went no further. The trailer had been here for some time, much longer than the bramble canopy because the foliage completely covered the metal chassis and wheels, hiding it from the world at large. Rust was highly evident across the entirety of the girders and struts that made up the design of the trailer

and the wheels had certainly seen better days, I doubted
that they would still turn. The tyres were flat and split
and the axles resembled one single lump of rust. I stared
in horror at this sight before shaking myself into life and
building my courage to face Mrs Hogh again. I needed
to ascertain what was to be done with this large rusted
trailer that nestled amongst a bed of thorns.

Some time later with my ears ringing I returned
to Bob and Trev with the news that the Hogh's wanted
the trailer removed. Blank faces stared back at me
following my news.

Bob scratched his head before muttering, 'How
the heck are we going to get that thing out?'

'We'll have to pull it out ourselves,' replied
Trev with absolutely no consideration for the fact that
the trailer was not only stuck fast in brambles and
rampant overgrowth, but its tyres were flat and the
wheels were rusted. The trailer was not going to move
from this spot easily; in fact I think it had begun to grow
roots itself.

After long moments contemplation I concluded
with a statement full of wisdom, 'It ain't going to
move.'

'So what are we going to do then – boss?'
enquired Bob with a malicious grin.

I did not fail to notice his exaggerated use of the word *boss* but choose to ignore it as I pondered the problem. Bob was delighting in reminding me that the responsibility was entirely on my shoulders and if anything went wrong it would be my fault, not his.

'Right. First of all, let's get this area cleared of brambles. Then we'll be able to see clearly what we're up against.'

'Up against a damn brick wall is what,' muttered Bob

'Bramble wall,' enjoined Trev.

'Stupid way to earn a living,' was Spike's only thought on the job in general.

Still muttering between themselves, they launched into battle again while I continued to stare in bewilderment at the huge lump of rust and rubber before me. It was not just that the trailer had seen better days; I also had to consider how we were going to manoeuvre it around the ninety degree angle that to reach the main road. Obviously the Hogh's had gotten the thing in so therefore I deduced with unusual clarity that if it came in, it must be able to get out. However at that moment in time I simply had no idea. I stared and stared but could reach no conclusion. Finally Bob became slightly agitated and thrust a pair of hedging shears into my hands with a definite suggestion I should do some damn work. Reluctantly I joined the assault of the brambles and waded in alongside Spike, Trev and Bob. With the aid of our own personal bulldozer, namely Trev, the area was soon cleared enough for us to re-evaluate the problem of removing the trailer. Then I had a bright idea. Strange for me I know but there it was: a solution.

'Back in a minute,' I told the others as I headed off to the house in order to use the phone. Remember, mobile phones are still relatively new devices and used mainly by that lost breed known as *Yuppies*. A term often used to describe those annoying individuals from the 1980's, the Young Upwardly–mobile Professionals. Back in those days ordinary peasants still had to use a landline to make a call. I had taken the option to phone a friend. My idea required the services of a good friend, a farmer type friend to be specific. A good farmer friend with a big tractor to be precise.

At the house I had to explain my plan and though Mr Hogh was somewhat doubtful, Mrs Hogh used her superior position in their relationship and gave me permission to go ahead. Quickly I made the phone call and then exited the property before Mrs Hogh could rage another attack on my ears. My plan was simple I hoped. I had asked my farmer friend is he would pop down with his tractor and pull the trailer out for me. He had replied that he would on condition that he could take it away for scrap. I paused to consider this request, just long enough to entice him further and ensure his rapid compliance. In truth I only wanted the thing gone and out of my way as soon as humanly possible, but I did not want to be faced with a typical farmers' judgement of time. So after a pause and a sigh to indicate my pretend reluctance, I agreed that he could have the trailer to dispose of as he wished. He was happy and I was happy. However I still had no idea if my plan would work and if we were going to get the thing out.

While we waited all three of us continued with other jobs around the garden as there was still much to do. I left Spike and Trev to clear all the cut brambles and dead Triffids into a pile in a corner of the bottom area beside where trailer lay rusting in peace. Bob and I returned to weeding, trimming and tidying in the main section of the garden.

Some thirty minutes later the farmer arrived, we could hear his tractor chugging along several minutes before he actually arrived on the road outside. We all stopped what we were doing and waited as the farmer reversed his tractor into the alley like lane. When he reached the ninety degree bend he stopped, turned off the tractor and jumped out.

'How do folks,' he greeted us with a smile, 'Sorry I'm bit late. One `o me cows fell down a bleddy hole and I `ad to shoot un.'

'Did you shoot it in the hole?' asked Bob.

'Nah, don't be thick man, I shot `un in the `ead!'

After that stupefying statement, the farmer looked at the bramble surrounded trailer and commented, 'Tis a hellva job ee's got on `ere boys ain't it.'

'Yeah we know. So can you get your tractor in enough to attach the trailer to it?' I asked when the formal and informal greetings were concluded.

'Yes I think so, maybe a bit tight but we'll do ee. You'll `ave to see me back, don't wanna scat down this `ere house.'

Off he went back to climb into the tractor and once more it roared, coughed and spluttered into life. Gingerly he began edging the machine around the sharp bend, inch by inch and with many minor three point turns the huge wheels slowly drew nearer to the trailer. Finally he was close enough to attach his tow hitch. This took some time and several curses as of course the trailer ball hitch was little more than rust. Plus most of the trailer was still covered with grass and other assorted grasping foliage so it took all five of us to prise the tow hitch from the ground and up high enough to reach the tractor tow bar.

At last the connection was made and the farmer returned to the tractor cab and gunned the engine. With a gesture to indicate he was ready to move, we all stepped back and watched with apprehension as the tractor was put into gear and the revs began to build. To our surprise and with all credit to the strength of the tractor, the trailer started to move almost immediately. The sound of ripping grass, tearing weeds and squashed gnomes filled the air as the trailer reluctantly moved forward. I was impressed by the unstoppable force of the agricultural machine as the trailer jerked and groaned nearer to the alley entrance.

'Ee'll 'ave to swing tha end round a bit ee knows. That thing ain't gonna go round this 'ere corner by hisself.'

Guided by the farmer's eloquent instructions, the four of us grasped a handhold on the trailer and bumped it around as the tractor chugged slowly on. We bumped, dragged, swore and forced the trailer into a position where the farmer could pull the rusted icon of a past boating age out of the garden. When all was lined up and ready to go, the farmer gave us a cheery wave and hauled the protesting trailer out from the alley and onto the road. Jumping down from his purring tractor, the farmer returned to ensure his work was done. I replied that it was and gave my thanks. The intelligent one amongst us posed a question to the farmer before he left.

'How are you going to manage to tow that thing on the road? Only one of the wheels is actually turning, won't you get in trouble if the police see you?'

'Nah. Them boys in blue is used to us farmers dragging all sorts of things round the countryside. They ain't gonna notice one more rusty wreck being towed. Anyway tis only a couple miles, no ones gonna even notice.'

The happy farmer jumped back into his cab and set off to where ever he planned to dispose of the rattling hunk of rust. I gave a few moments thought to his comments about no one noticing, I knew he was heading in the direction of a busy village and his route home was through the main street itself. The street would be full of shoppers and people going about their daily business. I felt sure some one would notice a grinning farmer on a huge tractor towing a squeaking, squealing, groaning and bumping along the narrow road. I kept my thoughts to myself. With the removal of the trailer work on the property of Mr and Mrs Hogh progressed at a sedate pace. Bob, Trev, Spike and I teamed up to conquer the unruly garden in good time. All the lawns had been cut, all shrubs and bushes had been trimmed and a healthy bonfire reduced the evidence to ashes on the area once owned by a rusting trailer.

The following day I arrived at the location slightly later as I had dropped Spike off at another property in order to avoid falling too far behind in my work bookings. I was greeted by a gloomy Bob who informed me that during the night Mr Hogh had quietly passed away. This of course was very sad news and I steeled myself to approach a distraught Mrs Hogh and offer my condolences. In the light of this distressing occasion Mrs Hogh and I decided to halt all work until after the funeral and the tying up of all legal requirements. Gathering up all our equipment we left Mrs Hogh to her grieving, promising to return and complete the work upon her request.

It was three weeks before I received the call from Mrs Hogh stating that she required us to continue

clearing and tidying her garden with the added request
that we now maintained the property on a regular basis
as she alone would not be able to cope. Rescheduling
my work rota, quite an easy task as the unfortunate
demise of Mr Hogh had left me with all four employees
and not enough work for them all. Consequently the
majority of my work list had been cleared in good time
and I now had some free time. Some days later Bob and
I returned to the Hogh residence to continue the job in
hand. As we arrived we were met by a strangely quiet
Mrs Hogh and she had a special request. He husband
had spent a lot of time in his shed during their married
years. I could empathise with her late husband as I
could picture his frequent retreat to the small wooden
structure at the side of the garden as a haven away from
the constant natter from Mrs Hogh. The request was that
we clear all her husband's tools and projects from the
shed as she felt they would be a constant reminder of
him and it would be upsetting. We were instructed to
leave only the gardening implements but dispose of all
other such tools and items as we saw fit. I admit to
being unhappy with this arrangement so I suggested that
we try and sell the tools and other items for her so she
would at least gain some financial benefit as she was
now a widow. Mrs Hogh reluctantly agreed to this but

in truth she was finding times hard. The legal process was of course taking its time and she was trying to manage on her small pension alone until the benefits of Mr Hogh's Will could be settled. A tearful Mrs Hogh informed us that her husband was properly insured and had accrued a good amount of savings which would become hers upon settlement of his Will. Until then her income remained small and she was struggling to cope. I was also upset at the recent events so it never occurred to me that I may not get paid if my customer was so financially restricted. Regardless I would not have been heartless enough to even broach the subject of money at that time so I agreed to continue working at her property.

So Bob and I carried on working on her garden and clearing her husband's shed as requested. Mr Hogh had quite a selection of tools and we managed to sell these easily, most men will always buy tools. In fact I bought some for myself as all were in excellent condition. Along with tools and other equipment I discovered two old outboard motors stashed at the rear of the shed. I knew nothing about the boating life or how to dispose of boat engines and the assortment of added equipment we found, such as a pair of oars, rollicks and fenders. After some discussion with Mrs

Hogh, her amicable nature had returned and she talked as much as ever, it was decided to contact a few boat owners for advice. My small area of the world was situated by the coast so this was not difficult.

Within a short time buyers had surfaced and the marine equipment was duly sold. The shed was finally bereft of all items not relating to gardening and Mrs Hogh had received a goodly sum to assist her as she await the settlement of her late husbands Will. All were happy upon this completion, Mrs Hogh at the removal of painful reminders and the income she had received. Bob and I were happy because it meant we could get on with what the firm of Green Fingers was all about, gardening.

Alas things were not to remain rosy with Mrs Hogh and her now gleaming garden. The Will and all the legal proceedings were still dragging on and though our work was now finished, poor Mrs Hogh did not have the ability to settle the final part of my bill. It had been arranged before her husband's demise that we would be paid on the completion of each task so the outstanding debt was not huge; in fact it was only a few days labour for me and Bob. Unfortunately this minor sum was too much for a cash strapped widow and with tears she informed me she could not pay. I felt terrible at this news. I was deeply sorry for Mrs Hogh's predicament but I was running a business and I had a family to feed and Bob to pay. Of course I sympathised with the poor woman and racked my brains in an attempt to discover a solution beneficial to both of us. It became evident that Mrs Hogh had thought long and hard on this issue herself and had a proposal for me.

With a sad face Mrs Hogh asked if I would take her husbands boat in lieu of payment for the last work completed. A boat! What the heck would I do with a boat! I had no interest or knowledge of boats and in a dumbfounded state I told Mrs Hogh that I would consider her proposal before answering. She then assured me that my services would still be required and that she would definitely hire my firm again once the Will had been settled. I thanked her for her promise of more business and repeated that I would seek advice before agreeing to take her late husbands boat. In truth I was totally out of my depth (please pardon the pun) and I left her property in confusion. I could afford to pay Bob as the business of Green Fingers was now profitable so when I told him of Mrs Hogh's suggestion, his apathy knew no bounds.

Some days later after finding the location of the offered vessel and accompanied by a sailing friend, I went in search of the boat to ascertain its value and decide if the deal was worth the cost of the work done. My friend was an enthusiastic sailor and his eagerness to view my in lieu of payment offer was considerable. So off we set one Saturday morning in search of a nautical adventure.

In a very small hamlet beside an estuary on mud moorings sat a pitiful looking Caprice 19. A wooden hulled twin keeled sailing boat of some age. A mast and boom were tied to its cabin roof and three sails were secured in a bag inside the vessel. Other items included a floating compass, twin bunks, a small gas cooker and a stained sink. As the Caprice was the twin keeled version, it sat sturdily upon the mud bank of a tiny inlet off the estuary itself. My friend described it as a Fractional Sloop, approximately nineteen foot long and just over six foot wide. The build material of the hull was plywood and was painted blue. The decks were white with pale blue anti-slip paint covering the areas were one waked, or staggered I concluded. All in all it resembled a floating, no wait, at the time of viewing it was not floating as the tide was out. For all I knew the damn thing would become a submarine with the incoming tide.

My sailing friend was over the moon in his delight at finding this vessel. With a wide grin he assured me this boat was well worth the money I was owed and that I should agree immediately. He faithfully promised to teach me to sail and help restore the sloop while he continued to peer under, over, in and out of the boat. It was obvious he was thrilled, I was still not convinced. I was sure this ancient looking boat was only good for Davey Jones locker. However I was finally talked into accepting this junior Titanic and on the following Monday I visited Mrs Hogh and accepted her offer. Suddenly as I drove away from her home I realised we had already sold off two outboard engines, oars and paraphernalia that accompanied the somewhat distressed sailing boat known as a Caprice 19. We had even disposed of the boats own road trailer!

Chapter Thirteen: Blind leading the Blind.

Often our customers requested particular styles for their gardens and especially the lawns. Most did not mind how the lawn was cut as long as it was cut, and not by themselves. Some however liked the cut of a rotary mower, others preferred a cylinder mower and one particular gentleman wanted a cricket style pitch. This person, whom I rarely met as all business was conducted via post or phone, insisted strongly that the lawn featured mow lines that stretched away from his bungalow's rear windows in the fashion of the lines seen on cricket or football pitches. This is relatively easy to achieve as the lines are created by mowing up and down the lawn in straight lines. Light itself creates the effect of lines, reflecting off the grass that is laid over by the action of the roller on the back of a mower. The blades of grass that lean away from the sun reflect the light back while the blades that are rolled towards the sun do not reflect light back to the position of the viewer. Simple! The lining of lawns is a commonly used technique and if one can push; pull or follow a mower in a relatively straight line; one will produce the desired effect. But not if one cannot see!

I owned at that time, a huge self powered lawn mower. This mower had a large heavy roller at the back and was perfect at leaving lawn lines. However it was self powered as I have already mentioned and my colleague on that day was Trev. Trev was a man of muscle and energy but handling a self propelled machine was outside his capabilities. It was not that Trev could not handle a self propelled mower; it was more the case of not wanting too. He preferred to use his muscles and was not inclined to bother with what he termed a lazy man's machine. The rear lawn was the larger of the two and it was the rear lawn that our customer wanted lines on, so Trev went to the cut the front lawn with our usual rotary mower, leaving me to tackle the rear lawn. I was quite happy with this as the rear lawn was flat and approximately square, two features not often found in our area of Britain where domestic lawns can resemble the side of a mountain.

Work was progressing nicely when something strange happened. I suddenly realised I could no longer see out of the corners of my eyes, my periphery vision had gone. All I could see on each side of me was a white mist, strange I thought but I remained unconcerned. After a short time I noticed the white mist was slowly moving across my eyes and I was now finding it slightly difficult to see. Unexpectedly bright coloured streaks began lining the white mist and my vision narrowed even further. Now I was beginning to panic, nothing like this had ever happened before. My shocked brain had at last realised something extraordinary was happening to my eyes, so before I lost my sight completely, I ran round the building and shouted for Trev to come and help. I was concerned about the customer's lawn and the fact he may not appreciated any lines in his prized lawn that resembled a fight in a spaghetti factory.

When Trev appeared I quickly explained that something was wrong with my eyes and I could no longer see clearly enough to mow in a straight line. Trev was still reluctant to use the big self propelled mower and its heavy rear roller so we compromised. I continued to actually drive the thing while Trev ran between the ends of the lawn and instructed me to either move to the left or to the right in order to keep the lines straight and parallel to each other. Talk about the blind leading the blind.

Finally we did manage to complete the lawn and Trev assured me that its appearance was good, the lines did not wobble too much and that the finished result was satisfactory. Trev then returned to finish the front lawn while I contemplated my onslaught of blindness and sat on garden bench with my head in my hands. Ten minutes of misery followed. Trev finished the front lawn and began clearing up and tidying. He loaded both mowers into the van, a fact I was always grateful for and now he was sipping at a cup of flask tea while awaiting the outcome of my unexpected blindness. I knew all this from the sounds made by Trev, he was certainly not the quietest of workers and each action was accompanied with grunts as he loaded the mowers, followed by slurping noises as he drank his tea. By now my vision was entirely misted, I could see vague impressions of the landscape around me but I could not clearly define any features. I could not even see my hands or feet. I continued to sit and ponder how I was going to get home and if I would need a white stick for the rest of my life.

Still wallowing in dejection I watched a small bird flutter down onto the freshly cut grass and begin pecking for insects. I watched that bird for several moments before I realised my eyes had cleared and my vision had returned to normal. Relief flowed through me as I comprehended the fact that I was not going blind after all, not at that moment anyway. I stood up and made my way around to the front of the property where my van was parked with the intention of departing the property with all due haste. I had no idea what made my vision react so strangely, and I resolved to visit my doctor and get myself checked out.

The next symptom occurred just as Trev and I made ourselves comfortable in the van and discussed whether to head for our next client and risk my blindness returning or head home immediately. Trev did not mind either way, he obviously wanted to continue working because he was paid by the hour, no work no pay. He also enjoyed punishing his body in that strange establishment known as a gym. We decided I had recovered so it was agreed that we would continue working. But as I grasped the steering wheel my head exploded! Not literally of course but that was how it felt.

'What's up with you? You've gone totally white and why are you swearing so much?' asked Trev with concern as I doubled up over the steering wheel in agony.

'It's my head! It's gonna burst. Bleddy hell it hurts! Can you drive Trev?'

'Sorry mate, I can't drive on the road legally, not got a licence. Can't you do it, you normally drive OK?'

'That's when I'm okay, not when I'm bleddy suffering you wally! Aaargghh! My head is splitting! Sod it, we're going home. If I can get us there that is. Bleddy hell!'

With a pain in my head I never experienced before I began the journey home. I had no idea what was happening to me but what I did know was driving a beat up old work van was certainly not helping. Trev wisely remained quiet during the home journey, aside from the occasional warning of a bus or truck heading straight for us and recommending frantically that I steer out of the way. It was several miles to the safety of my home, mainly through narrow country lanes littered with tractors, holiday makers who did not have the ability to reverse and the occasional kamikaze deer. Finally the torturous journey ended and I arrived at my home and virtually fell from the van, still in absolute agony. Trev also exited the van though relief at making it through the journey alive clearly showed on his face.

'What are you doing home?' asked my wife who had been tending our own front garden.

When the trembling had subsided enough to talk, Trev made the understatement of the decade, 'He's got a bit of a headache I think.'

I could have killed him but it would have hurt my head too much, I wobbled over to my wife and between groans and cusses I slowly, very slowly lowered myself down onto the grass. Arms folded tightly across her chest, my wife stood over me and demanded an explanation in a totally unsympathetic tone. Almost in a whisper and punctuated with expletives I explained the problem.

'Oh you're probably having a migraine, that's all,' she replied with a frown. 'When did it come on?'

I could only groan in reply so Trev filled in the details, trying hard not to laugh as these sorts of situations often seem quite funny to onlookers. My wife looked down at where I was still sat with my head in my hands, frightened to move as every minor movement of my body seemed to jar my head. Even my rapidly beating heart thumped inside my head like an unskilled rabid drummer in a punk band. Placing her hands under my arms, my wife gently helped me to my feet and led me up the garden path, something she has done on many occasions since.

'Go indoors and I'll get some painkillers. Sorry Trev, but you may as well head off home as well. I don't think he'll be doing any more work today.'

Trev set off giving an over cheerful wave, which I hated him for as my wife helped me stagger into the house. Movement, daylight and each step rattled my head with such pain I did not know whether to throw up or give up.

Since then I have had several of these charming headaches. A trip to the doctor the next day informed me that I had suffered an aura migraine; hence the temporary loss of vision and zigzag lines being followed by an exploding head. I now recognise the signs and when ever my vision begins to fade, I run though slowly and screaming though quietly to the medicine cabinet. Luckily the customer never knew his lawn had been mown by a blind man following instructions from a non-mechanical fitness enthusiast, and we never admitted otherwise. Chalk up yet another new experience in the life of a mobile gardener.

Chapter Fourteen: Obsession

It must be said that some gardeners can be quite obsessed with the appearance and overall neatness of their gardens; some it seems place more importance on maintaining a horticultural standard than may be considered normal. However when this obsession is twined with inconsideration, the situation then has a habit of becoming incomprehensible.

My business had been running for some time now and it was turning out to be reasonably successful. I had even managed to arrange time off for me to enjoy a holiday at home with my wife and children. Due to the seasonal aspect of my work, I could not afford to take time off during the spring, summer and autumn periods, so the only option left was winter. I did not mind this as it was a price I was willing to pay in order to get my business off the ground so to speak. A slight pun perhaps as my business involved the ground itself, what was in it, growing on it and even above it in fact. I decided I would take a full two weeks holiday at – Christmas. Lucky me! I planned to stop work when the schools closed for the holiday break, a period that ranged between two and three weeks, depending on which Council officer had the staff calendar that day.

Many times people sunning themselves on holiday while I was slogging behind a hot mower had enquired where I take my holidays. When I replied that I usually took two weeks over Christmas, their noses turned up with distain. They obviously considered a lowly gardener could not afford such as grand holiday as they were enjoying, on a caravan site amidst screaming children, barking and crapping dogs and drunken adults. To relieve the boredom of chasing a noisy, smelly petrol lawn mower around all day, I would often reply that I took my holidays in the Algarve or skiing in the Alps. That usually shut them up!

I kept myself busy during the winter with cleaning greenhouses, repairing and painting garden sheds, up rooting unwanted hedges, shrubs or trees and laying as many patios as I could. I even offered any customer ten percent off the total price of a patio if they had it done during the winter months. Most gardeners, hobbyists or professionals alike, leave their gardens alone during winter, hibernating themselves in potting sheds, pubs or in front of the television. As I was keen to build my business and having a family that required supporting, I chose to continue working throughout the year, including the winter months. It was hard because people rarely consider their gardens over winter and happily forget all those little jobs they had to do, only to discover those same jobs still waiting to done in spring. So keeping a gardening business running through winter was a difficult chore but I was managing. I mostly worked on my own, not having the work or the income to employ Bob or Trev over winter. Both were quite happy with this arrangement, neither liked the cold and much preferred the warmth of home or pub, or the gym in Trev's case. I did call on either or both of them when I did manage to obtain work laying a patio or some other chore that I could not handle on my own, but the work was not constant enough to deem the presence of a full time employee. It was not that they had no work at all, it was rather the case of reduced hours as by then I did have enough work to ensure at least one or two days work for who ever had the misfortune to be available to work for me at that time. Mainly I worked through winter on my own, weeding in icy conditions, climbing trees in gale force winds and clearing leaves and other assorted garden debris from the wet and soggy ground.

However now it was Christmas and I felt I was entitled to enjoy the festive season with my wife and two young children, a wish every father has, even if just to sneak a secret play with the children's toys. Christmas arrived on a bright and sunny but very cold day. I was busy with the children opening their presents with varying degrees of delight. I had learned very early in fatherhood not to buy clothes for a little boy at Christmas, so both my children seemed content with the sack loads of presents from Father Christmas. One of my children did make a comment that it would be nice to get a present from us parents, instead of leaving every thing to Santa. My wife had retreated to the kitchen in order to prepare our religious festive meal, otherwise know as a burnt offering. But apart from that, our Christmas day was proceeding happily, until the phone rang.

It was Mrs Pollard-Brown the vicar's wife and the last person I expected to hear from today, Christmas Day of all days. With a slight cough to clear her throat, Mrs Pollard-Brown asked what time I would be arriving to tend her garden. This Christmas Day had fallen on a Tuesday and it was normally the Tuesday of each week that I visited her property. At first I could not speak, I was in shock. Who would need a gardener on Christmas Day? Especially a vicar's wife! Surely she was not serious I thought. But she was, in fact she was adamant that I attend her garden and do some tidying as she had guests arriving later in the day and wanted the garden to look its best.

Then followed a lengthy and slightly surreal phone conversation, Mrs Pollard-Brown insisting I come out on Christmas Day and tidy her garden. I was refusing stubbornly, stating that I was not going to leave my family on this particular day of the year and that my children would never forgive me. I even reminded her that Christmas Day was a religious day when we all celebrated the birth of Jesus. She retorted that she was well aware of this fact and reminded me yet again that her husband was a vicar and he had to work that day. I bit my tongue and did not retort that he chose his profession and a couple of hours work in the morning did not constitute too much of a hardship. Instead I continued to refuse as politely as I could while my two children shouted for daddy to come back and play with them.

With desperation in her voice Mrs Pollard-Brown offered to pay me extra if I attended her garden. I will admit I did consider this as a few extra pounds earned was always handy, especially at Christmas. After some moments thought I came to my senses and decided to play Mrs Pollard-Brown at her own game. I requested five hundred pounds for two hours work tidying her already immaculate garden. The phone went silent, I could tell she was actually giving the request some thought. Finally she also came to her senses and declined, adding that she would expect my presence at the very moment the Christmas holiday period ended. I assured her I would be there, wished her and her husband a happy Christmas and said good bye. I then returned to the organised chaos that is Christmas Day in a family with two young children and the threat of mother-in-law arriving hanging over the joyful proceedings.

To this very day I still cannot understand why on Christmas Day of all days, a vicar's wife had felt the desperate need for a tidy garden and would expect a family man to leave his young children and do the work. What ever happened to Christian charity and good will to all men? This was a fine concept in principle, but certainly not as important to Mrs Pollard-Brown as having a neat garden. I did of course visit Mrs Pollard-Brown as soon as the festive season was over. Nothing more was said about her Christmas Day phone call and nor did she appear to hold any grudge against me. Personally I think her husband may have said something when he learned what she had planned. What ever the reason, it was not mentioned again and I continued to maintain Mrs Pollard-Brown's property for many years.

Chapter Fifteen: Strange Phobia

In the course of my time gardening I meet many different customers, most were almost normal, like the bored retired gentleman and the very rich lady, a minister's wife, the odd famous person and several others of whom I considered dubious. However one of the most surprising behavioural habits of a customer came to light when we were contracted to lay a crazy paved patio for a retired couple living in a small community of homes on what was once a farm. This collection of residents sat like an island of humanity in a wilderness of agriculture, surrounded by fields and woodlands and at least two miles from any other civilisation.

On this day, it was Spike who accompanied me as we set off to estimate and organise the area to be paved. It was winter and we were both wrapped up like polar explorers. Neither of us were eagerly awaited the freezing wind that cut deeply through even the thickest of clothing. It took some time to locate the property as it was so tucked away behind a screen of trees. In fact I drove past it twice before noticing the large sign standing prominently beside the entrance road to the dozen or so homes nestling within. Like I said, it was deep winter and my mind was definitely feeling the chill, so it was very easy to miss a huge sign jutting out into the road. Finally however we did arrive at the correct address and reluctantly climbed out from the warm interior of the van, to be met on their doorstep by the elderly couple, Mr and Mrs Robin who required our services.

The area to be paved was not large, in fact it was quite small and a fact I was grateful for, because laying crazy paving can drive one insane. Imagine assembling a thousand piece puzzle while standing in a fridge and each piece had jagged and totally random edges. Crazy paving ranks amongst the highest of tedious activities, laying one in winter was the icing on the cake, ice being the operative word here. The ground on which the paving was to be laid consisted of patchy and scruffy grass, many weeds and bare areas. We had also been charged with erecting a small wall round the area so obviously our first task was to clear all the vegetation and dig out a trench for the wall foundations. As the area was so small and the wall was to be only a couple of feet or sixty centimetres high, the foundations were not dug deep. The frozen ground however turned this simple task into a major exertion, pick axes and shovels bouncing off the iron ground. It took a day longer than I had hoped but I was not really worried, it was winter and work was scarce so we felt no need to hurry as we made sure all was correctly prepared for the wall and the paving that was to follow.

I had noticed during this time that Mrs Robin vanished from sight as soon as me or Spike grasped a pick axe or a spade. I gave this insignificant fact little thought at the time, I was too busy trying to figure out how to mix and lay cement in such cold conditions. Once upon a time a wise old builder had informed me that cement should not be laid in temperatures less than four degrees Celsius. Makes sense I suppose, frozen concrete does not spread well. I did not know the actual temperature that day but figured the icicles hanging from my nose might suggest it was a tad cold.

I must point out that we charged by the actual working hour, so if we were held up by ice, snow, blizzards or any other form of biblical disaster it did not cost our customer a penny extra. I believe the term is *Piecemeal*, we only charged for time worked. So if we worked one hour, we charged one hour. Of course this made sense as British winters, and summers come to that, are renowned for irrational weather patterns and mostly this concerned the levels of rain we received. On this particular job we were forced to take our time due

to the freezing conditions. Not discounting frozen
fingers, toes and rock hard ground.

Work eventually came to a halt when the cold
turned to rain. Frozen ground became soggy ground and
this caused another short delay. The joys of working
outside in winter! In due course the weather settled and
we began the work in earnest. Not that we were working
in earnest, in fact I do not even know where Earnest is.
Quickly we finished the trench for the wall foundations,
laid and levelled the cement base and began to erect the
wall that was to serve as a boundary between the patio
and the road. The elderly gentleman, Mr Robin, spent
much of his time watching and chatting to us as we
worked. He was a likeable man with a full head of no
hair, metal rimmed glasses and a round cheerful face.
Quiet spoken and constantly armed with mugs of tea
and plates of biscuits, his presence became a constant
factor while we worked. We saw little of Mrs Robin
outside, however she too chatted to us constantly by
leaning out her kitchen window. She rarely ventured
outside unless it was to get into their motorcar and head
off for the shops or some other errand. The short trip to
the vehicle was by way of a long plastic sheet, laid
down by her husband and it stretched from her front

door all the way to the door of their car. I will admit this behaviour puzzled me slightly. She was obviously a cheerful and friendly lady and appeared to enjoy conversing with us while we worked. She was certainly not watching us for our manly attractions.

At that time of the year we had so many clothes on. Including woolly hats with the health and safety regulated hard hats clamped on top so we resembled walking jumble sales rather than Adonises. I have never understood why one should be required to wear a safety hard hat when one is working on the ground. It is not as if a section of broken paving slab was going to suddenly shoot up into the air before falling down upon our heads. But as an employer I had to adhere to these strange health and safety rituals. However concerning the reluctance of Mrs Robin, I failed to understand why she never left the house while we were working outside it. Eventually I would discover the surprising reason.

That day had dawn bright and though cold, it was not nearly as cold as it had been. In fact it could be termed as fresh rather than cold. Spike and I had stripped off at least one coat from our layers due to the slight increase in temperature. Unfortunately laying a crazy paved area is not labour intensive enough to cause a sweat. Fiddling around with odd shaped pieces of concrete slab and attempting to get them to fit together is a greater strain on the brain than the body so we were still cocooned in layers of warm clothing. As usual Mr Robin was stood on his doorstep watching us work. Occasionally he would assist by pointing out a particular piece of slab that may fit in the area where we knelt on our giant jigsaw puzzle. Other than that the conversation continued as normal. Cosmology, rocket science, brain surgery and the true meaning of life are of course the usual subject's men cover during idle conversation, but on that morning we were discussing much deeper concerns. The topics being covered included the waste of space otherwise known as the government, do we need religion and the state of modern motor vehicles. Luckily the very difficult subject of women did not arise, I was married and would not dare, Mr Robin was elderly and his wife was within earshot and Spike declined that subject in fear of the customer and me becoming maudlin and jealous. Spike still being a single man that is. I felt he should stop being happy and get married like the rest of us.

Both Spike and I were on the ground trying to fit each piece of slab fragment in place when I was forced to grab a trowel and remove a small mound of earth that protruded higher than the ground around it. From the corner of my eye I noticed Mrs Robin quickly step back from the window from which she had watched us work. Wondering what caused such a rapid movement in someone of mature years, I mentioned it to her husband who ventured out to stand near us.

'Oh there's nothing to worry about, my wife suffers from Scoleciphobia. She's terrified of worms and cannot bear to be in the vicinity of loose soil in case one should pop up.'

Now this statement, made in such a nonchalant tone and with a straight face would have normally sent Spike and me into peals of laughter. However as our customer was paying us, we both forced down the mirth and hide our emotions from our faces.

'That's unusual; don't think I've heard of that one before. What about you Spike, have you heard of that?'

Spike glanced at me viciously; he was desperately trying to avoid an out right laugh, 'No, never,' he eventually replied.

'That's not surprising, though there are many suffers of this phobia, most manage to hide it quite well. Nearly all chose a career in offices or retail, anything in fact that helps them avoid encountering worms,' Mr Robin explained.

Suddenly I felt ashamed, and peering over at Spike I noticed he too was experiencing feelings of guilt. My mind had flashed up an image of my own fear, an irrational fear in the British Isles but one many people experience. I hate spiders and I knew Spike did also. Most men attempt to hide this fear, acting in bravado when a wife, girlfriend or mistress draws their attention to a spider in the bath. It is an Urban Myth that all men are unafraid of spiders. When there are no witnesses in the vicinity, many men run squealing like a child when a spider is encountered. In the majority of households, it is the woman who has to deal with arachnids, not the husband, boyfriend or neighbour hiding in the wardrobe. I freely admit any spider larger than a Money spider or Sheet Weaver as it is also known, will send shivers down my spine, however my absolute biggest hate is the Earwig. I once unwittingly slept right next to a nest. I awoke during the night covered from head to toe in the damn things! I have also enjoyed the pleasure of being *pinched* by one of these little horrors, and it hurt worse that a wasp sting. So it is no wonder I hate this insect so and avoid them at all costs. Not quite a phobia, more of a loathing but not as scary as a spider!

Therefore Spike and I felt empathy with our lady customer, even though the thought of being scared of a lowly earth worm seemed extremely unreasonable to us. At that point I noticed there were no flowers beds at all on the property. Numerous flower pots and tubs overflowed with Polyanthus and daffodils while Wall flowers (*Erysimum*) awaiting the spring. The customer noticed my glances and with a smile, decided to explain.

'Obviously having a fear of worms mean we cannot have any dug or loose soil like flower beds in the garden. So we use pots, tubs and containers to grow things and I have to sift all the soil and compost for worms before putting it in the containers. Once that is done my wife is happy to plant, water and care for the flowers and do the weeding whilst knowing there are no dastardly earth worms (*Oligochaeta*) waiting to savagely attack her.'

'That makes sense,' I replied, 'pity we can't get rid of spiders the same way!'

'Spiders? Surely you are not afraid of spiders? We don't have any nasty species in our country so why are you afraid of spiders?' asked the customer disbelievingly.

'Dunno,' I muttered, 'maybe for the same reason your wife doesn't like the harmless earth worm.'

'Ahh. Point taken. I'm sorry. Well it is a strange world. Here we are in a country with very few harmful creatures and many of us, if not all of us find ourselves afraid of the most humble creatures. Personally I would hate to encounter a Cobra or a Grizzly bear or even a Black Widow spider for that matter, fears that I think are well founded. But it amazes me just how many things living or inert, can frighten people.'

'Yep, have you met the wife? She frightens me!' I replied with a grin.

That concluded our strange but enlightening conversation and the talk returned to more mundane issues of the modern world.

It was some days later when we saw the first real sign of our lady customers fear. We were all sat out on the completed section of crazy paved patio enjoying tea and biscuits and eyeing up the rest of the area to be paved. The area we were working on had been covered in a layer of fine building sand as a base on which to lay the pieces of slab, so there were no signs of any vicious and nasty worms to frighten poor Mrs Robin. Unfortunately we had not yet covered the entire area with sand and a large section near the front door step remained as bare earth, but as yet no worm had dared poke its head out from its warm soil home. It is possible a few worms had attempted to scale the heights of freedom and reach the surface; however we had previously packed down the ground hard to ensure the newly laid slabs would not move about on their bed of sand. The hard packed ground may also ensure any upwardly mobile worms would only achieve a headache.

'Anyone for tea?' came Mrs Robin's voice from her kitchen doorway.

'Yes please,' was our combined response.

Gingerly Mrs Robin stepped out from the door with a laden tray held tightly in her hands. On it rested three steaming mugs of tea and a plate stacked high with yet more assorted biscuits. I wondered at that point if the Robins' had shares in a well known biscuit factory. Quickly Mr Robin moved to collect the tray however it appeared his frightened wife was going to be brave. With a determined expression she stepped completely out the door and stood upon the door step, a matter of inches from the uncovered soil.

I was concerned, knowing the unpredictability of nature, I fully expected a vicious worm to erupt from the ground and send Mrs Robin into screams of terror. My eyes scanned the surface of the ground in her vicinity, hoping to nail any wanton invertebrate attack on this poor defenceless lady. I need not have worried, not one timid worm decided to explore the surface world at that time and Mrs Robin stepped down onto the bare earth. What happened next shocked me to my core. The bravery of the woman was plain for all to see. Each step reflected in fear upon her face, her whole body was rigid and the tray of refreshments shock as her hands trembled. Quickly we all grasped a mug of tea and a couple of biscuits, anxious that Mrs Robin return to the safety of her home as soon as possible.

Now I know most of you are expecting a worm to appear and send Mrs Robin screaming for sanctuary in her kitchen. Well this did not happen. Once we all held our tea and biscuits, Mrs Robin returned to her home and her regular position at the kitchen window. I gave a sigh of relief, accompanied I noticed by a similar sigh from her husband. Spike of course was hoping for a show, in fact I was surprised he did not have a worm or two secreted in a pocket, ready to be planted at her unsuspecting feet. But no, even Spike would not be that mean and deep down I think he too was grateful that Mrs Robin had escaped her personal horror, especially after her extremely brave effort to play the host and supply us with refreshments.

It was a lucky escape. No sooner had Mrs Robin entered her home when Mr Robin gently poked me in the ribs. As I turned to face him, he discreetly pointed out not one, not two but four worms that had surfaced only inches from where Mrs Robin had stood. Of course we did not enlighten her.

Some weeks of dodging the British weather brought the job to its completion. I am happy to report there were only a few occurrences of worm attacks and Mrs Robin duly entertained us with the speed with which she exited the offending area. However these episode were few and our biggest problem in completing the crazy paved patio remained the winter conditions, the odd sneak attack of frost bite, loss of circulation in fingers and toes and a head ache from trying to assemble hundreds of broken pieces of paving slab into an aesthetically pleasing feature of modern horticultural preference.

Chapter Sixteen: Memories.

I ran the small landscaping and garden maintenance business known as Green Fingers for over twelve years before finally coming to my senses. Whenever I arrived at a prospective new customer's property I was always filled with anticipation. Would I discover a friend for life or a fiend, a relaxed and easy going individual or a tyrant? By now my business was established so I no longer needed to cope with tyrants and those awkward customers. I now had the delightful ability to pick and choose who I would work for, a situation that certainly lifted ones spirits when setting out on a spring day to provide work estimates and encounter new faces. The vast majority of my paying customers were elderly and I greatly enjoyed knowing them. I also had a high proportion of businesses on my work sheet, from caravan sites to garages and even the local doctors' surgery called on me occasionally.

When working for one local doctor I did have cause to require her services. We had been charged with demolishing an old but large garden shed. No problem there initially as we often undertook tasks relating to garden structures such as sheds, greenhouses and outbuildings. I only provided services that were attached to a garden, I would paint a garden shed but not the house, I would wax a garden seat but not house furniture. In fact I refused all requests that did not relate to horticulture in some way, I ensured I remained a gardener and did not become an odd job man.

The shed was leaning precariously at the bottom of her reasonable sized garden, lined on one side by compost bins and on the other side, uncomfortably close to the dilapidated shed stood a green house. Our instructions were to demolish the shed in a manner that would not damage the greenhouse, so I decided to take it apart bit by bit. Unfortunately I had not considered just how old and rotten it was. Carefully Bob and I first removed the double doors at the front of the shed, and then we removed all guttering and windows. The guttering was especially easy as it was on the point of collapse anyway. It was about that time when we realised that maybe we should empty out the contents of the shed before going any further. It had been a hard day and that is my excuse.

When the shed stood as an empty husk, the work of demolishing it began in earnest. With the aid of a specialised tool, a large sledge hammer, I decided to smash out the tongue and grove slats from either side of the door way. With a mighty swing the hammer hit the

intended slat - and the shed fell down! I had not
intended this to happen of course, but the whole
structure simply collapsed in a heap. It did not wobble
or fall to one side, it did not shake or slide, it just
collapsed. With me under it!

The world went black, with some shades of
brown and green. The air became full of dust and
cobwebs and insects scurried for their lives, all over me.
Within moments I felt hands grasping my coat collar
and I was dragged kicking and screaming from the
wreckage, I hate spiders and they were crawling in
unwanted places about my person. Once clear of the
now fully demolished shed, Bob left me lying on the
grass while he rushed to the house and called for the
doctor. Finally she came out, wiping her hands on a
small towel and stared down at my prone form.

'Make an appointment with the surgery to see
me later,' she said as she turned her back on my pathetic
prone figure and returned to her house. And that was the
extent of her professional medical treatment on that day.

Not all my years working as a mobile gardener,
landscaper and shed demolisher were as uneventful as
that day believe it or not. Sometimes we even had what
might be termed as bad luck. I had used a variety of

beaten up work vans for transporting the equipment along with sandwiches and a tea flask to and from jobs, but until now I had not bothered with any form of advertising on the sides of the vans. However upon taking possession of yet another van I decided it may be good for business if I had the name of Green Fingers and a phone number written on the van to promote my business. I duly contacted a local sign writer firm and decided on the modern computer generated stick on vinyl lettering in broad white characters along with a logo. This did turn out to be a wise move as my business increased by approximately thirty percent that year, after an unfortunate and embarrassing incident that is.

Bob and I were on our way to a prospective new customer in the van displaying the new livery that proclaimed the business name and phone number to all and sundry. I remember I had even washed the van early that morning and now it gleamed in the sunshine as we forced our way like kamikaze pilots through the summer holiday traffic. Our spirits were high and all was well with the world. Eventually we turned in to the large housing estate where the customer lived and began searching the house numbers in order to locate the property. Identifying the correct road in amongst the lines and lines of houses, we made a turn on to the road – and the van broke down!

The small housing estate of our prospective customer was obviously one of middle class residents, well kept gardens, highly maintained and shiny houses, at least two vehicles on each drive and people walking around in golfing attire. Amidst this scene of suburban perfection was my van, broken down and stuck in the middle of a weed free and clean swept road. My beaten old van, clean as it was stood out like a politician at a lie detector convention. Curtains twitched, heads appeared round corners and eyes stared in horror that this lump of scrap metal clutter sat slightly smoking on their tidy road. Worse still were the two scruffy individuals that climbed out of the van and scratched their heads while muttering curses and abuse at the stationary vehicle.

I tried in vain to restart the damn thing but to no avail, so finally I had to phone one of the road rescue companies to come out and either fix the van or tow it home. It was definitely not a good start to the day. The person on the phone stated that the man from the recovery company would take at least thirty minutes to reach us so instead of lounging in the vehicle, I decided to visit our possible new customer and give an estimate for the work required. I should not have bothered. The property was only a hundred or so yards up the road and it was not long before I stood on his door step and pushed the little door bell button. By the time the chimes had finished, the door opened and I was met by an elderly gentleman in the standard issue of fawn trousers, fawn soft loafers, a fawn cardigan over a crisp white shirt all topped by a sour expression.

'Yes? Can I help you,' said the gentleman from his doorway. I noticed he did not open the door fully and neither did he let go of it. His whole body language suggested deep embarrassment accompanied with the desire to flee this uncouth ragamuffin stood untidily on his polished door step.

'You called in connection with some gardening work? I am from Green Fingers. How may we help?'

'Is that thing yours?' he asked while gesturing in distain at my poor van that was now leaking oil in a puddle on the very clean road.

'Er. Yes it is. Unfortunately it has broken down this morning and I am waiting for the recovery man to arrive.'

'Yes well. I'm afraid I cannot possibly have something like that littering our road. One also wonders if you gentleman are actually qualified to undertake chores on my property. Therefore I feel I must decline your services. I am sorry for wasting your time,' replied the fawn gentleman with a sniff and a surreptitious glance about the estate in the futile hope that none of his neighbours were watching.

'My van is a tool for work and like any machine it can fail occasionally. The fact that it has broken down does not in any way reflect upon our horticultural services. It may also help to further establish the fact that I am a gardener, not a mechanic, my expertise are in horticulture and botany and my work is of the highest standard,' I replied indignantly as he began to swing his door closed.

'I am very sorry. Good bye,' he concluded as the door finally shut, leaving me dumbfounded and quite insulted.

OK, I admit I told a few fibs about the experience in horticulture and especially botany, as far as I was concerned, botany was a bay in Australia. I jest but one should not admit ones failings, it is not good for business.

However as I have already said, my business was doing well and luckily I did not have to worry about the petty and snobbish opinions of one person. I did however regret having the sign writing placed on my van that morning. In due course the rescue van arrived and after some tinkering, prodding and examining, the repairman decided my vehicle was in need of the tender care of a mechanic in a garage. So not only did I lose a customer that morning, I also had to suffer the humiliation of my van with its resplendent sign writing declaring to the world in general, my business name and my phone number, being towed off to a garage. This form of advertising I could do without.

I did eventually get three customers on that would be posh estate, one of which was directly across the road (with oil stain) from the image fanatic fawn gentleman, how ever he never acknowledged me and I did not acknowledge him, an arrangement I was quite satisfied with. The three customers I did obtain turned out to be normal human beings and cared not a jot for the condition of my van. It has never failed to amaze me how some people can fill themselves with so much self importance they eventually shut themselves off from the majority of the human population. In truth many of my customers could be classed as wealthy, some were even famous, one or two were certainly infamous but they paid well so who was I to judge. I occasionally enjoyed the patronage of the rich though not too often unfortunately. I was contracted by one particular very wealthy or rich lady who owned a six bedroom house but only used it as a holiday home. I maintained this property for well over eight years but only saw her twice. She actually lived in Australia but had family who lived locally and who looked after the house itself on her behalf. It was redecorated regularly, the expensive motor car kept in her garage was serviced and tested and taxed, cleaned and polished gleaming in readiness for her visits but she never came. On the two occasions I did get to meet her, she had decided on a six week holiday in England, I found her very pleasant and certainly generous. She once tipped me to the value of two days work for simply carrying her bag from the taxi to her front door. Like I said, a really lovely lady and it was a pity she only visited her holiday home so infrequently.

There is one particular garden that remains in my memory but not for its horticultural designs, nor its large lawns or the colourful shrubberies, ornamental trees or thick lush hedges. As can be deduced from the description, it was indeed a lovely garden and I enjoyed my fortnightly visits. It did however have one slight drawback, the garden was haunted! Now before all you sceptics fall about laughing hysterically, do not knock it until you can actually prove the non-existence of ghosts, ghouls, supernatural nasties and honest politicians. Personally I chose to keep an open mind, I have never physically seen a billion pounds but I know such a thing does exist. In the dreams of myself and countless others of course, but a billion pounds does exist though actually seen by very few.

So who is to say whether my claim to that haunted garden is true or otherwise? At some time or another, Bob, Spike and even Trev experienced something odd while working there, so it was not just the workings of my inactive mind trying to find something to do and relieve its boredom. However did we in reality see a ghost? I do not think so; it was more of a presence that accompanied us in our work around the garden. My experience was that of being followed and watched constantly. I found myself constantly looking over my shoulder expecting someone to be there. Sometimes when I was engrossed in the mindless routine of mowing the large but luckily, quite flat lawns, the perception that someone was walking directly towards me would cause me to lift my head and fully open my eyes, only to find no one there. Other times I would be convinced someone was talking to me, other than the usual voices in my head that is. These days my schizophrenia does not bother either of us quite so much. Anyway, on several occasions one of my colleagues would come running in a slow walk fashion, over to where I was working and ask what I wanted. When I enquired as to what they were talking about, they would reply that they thought I had called to them. But by far the worst sensation was when I was on my hands and knees weeding a patch of flower bed and I could swear someone was on their knees beside me. But of course no one was there.

I had enquired as to the history of the property from the present owners but no one knew of any strange happenings in the past that may account for these odd sensations. In truth the owners had only moved into our area in the last few years and knew little if any thing about the location or its people or the local history. The only thing they did venture as information was the fact that they had buried their deceased cat beneath one of the Willow trees, but I am sure it was not a cat that haunted us. All of us who had witnessed this tale of the unexpected were convinced our friendly gardening enthusiast from the other side was an elderly gentleman. Perhaps he was checking our work, making sure the garden remained in a condition that suited his ghostly wanderings. Or mayhap he was trying to communicate with us, shouting that we were doing something wrong or working too slow. Who ever he was, if he did not keep frightening the life out of us, we would have been able to work faster!

From the sublime to the ridiculous, another memory concerns not the garden owners themselves but the very annoying botanist who lived next door. Bob and I were working on the property of an elderly lady called Mrs Lowry, it was a cold spring that year and we were giving her garden a total overhaul. Flower beds were removed and put to grass, shrubs were ripped out and her small pond was dug out and the resulting hole was filled in. Not a sensible idea to leave a whopping great hole in someone's garden, especially that of an old lady. We had completed most of the chores to the accompaniment of Mrs Lowry and her constant instructions and so called helpful advice. I was getting rather fed up with trying to please this cantankerous woman, who seemed to find fault in everything we did. She reminded me of a teacher I once had the dubious pleasure of knowing at school, I did not listen to her much either.

It was as we were coming to the final chore on Mrs Lowry's property when I discovered the reason behind her constant criticism; her nearest neighbour was a botanist. Each and every task we undertook on the property was scrutinised and commented on by the neighbour as soon as we had left at the end of each day. Now it must be pointed out that a botanist and a horticulturalist are two very different animals. It is true that both are concerned with the Kingdom of plants, however the botanist understands the biology, species, family and genetic make up of plants. A horticulturalist understands how to prepare the ground, plant the flowers and shrubs and how to lay and cut lawns. So this botanist fellow was becoming quite a pain, a thorn in my side if you wish. His knowledge came from a classroom while mine came from experience of actually doing the job. Yes, by now I was quite experienced; I had gained a lot of knowledge since my initial start in the business. I quickly resented the neighbour and his interference. His text book knowledge and academic learning held little sway in the very real practice of gardening. Bob described him as a 'wannabe' gardener who did not want to dirty his hands. I described him as a lazy begger who was qualified in interference.

The final job required of us was to plant a long line of Escallonia hedging down one side of Mrs Lowry's rear garden. The work went well as we prepared a long trench down the length of the garden in readiness for the insertion of young Escallonia saplings. The earth was fertilised, dug over several times and all traces of weed removed. Each sapling was carefully inserted into the ground and a small stake was tied to them to help against the wind. On the first day we managed to plant a dozen saplings after completing the ground preparation before it was time to leave work for the day.

When we returned the following day we found to our horror that several of the Escallonia saplings appeared to have been trodden down, while others lay scattered about, obviously having been ripped from the ground. We were dumbfounded and as we stood scratching our heads, Mrs Lowry appeared and began berating us for our poor workmanship. Avoiding the almost overwhelming desire to plant Mrs Lowry headfirst in the soil alongside the remaining saplings, we set about clearing and repairing the damage.

We completed the job later that day and finished our time with Mrs Lowry. Receiving our grudgingly offered payment, we set off, already planning the next day's work. However early the very next day I received an irate phone call from Mrs Lowry informing me that several of the Escallonia plants were laying on the ground and others had been snapped off at the stem. I reminded her that she had meticulously inspected our work before she finally paid the day before. I asked her in as polite a tone as I could manage, how the line of young Escallonia hedging had managed to become damaged over night. To this she had no answer. Dutifully Bob and I returned to her property before moving on the tackle our next job that day. Upon arrival we were met by another neighbour, a lady who lived on the other side of Mrs Lowry. The neighbour gestured from her front door to gain our attention so we walked over to her.

'Do you know what he's doing each evening?' she asked in a whisper.

'Know what who's doing' I questioned in a matching low voice.

'That man who lives the other side of Mrs Lowry, that's who. Do you know what he's up to?'

'No I'm sorry; I have no idea what you are saying. What is he up to each evening?'

'Well, Mrs Lowry tends to go to bed quite early each night. As soon as her lights go out, that man sneaks into her garden and tramples that hedge you've laid.'

'Oh that's what's been happening. I'll have to have a chat with him later. Thank you for the information and I'll make sure it doesn't happen again. Believe me.'

Concluding the conversation with the neighbour, Bob and I returned to Mrs Lowry's garden and once more repaired the damage. Mrs Lowry did not rant and rave at us as I had expected, instead she appeared quite upset and worried about the strange happenings in her garden. I did not let on that I knew the reason. I have long known that if you try to inform some one that a person they consider a close friend is in fact a total miscreant, the person informed is just as likely to turn on you. So I said nothing but, I had a cunning plan.

That evening, just as darkness was creeping across the land, I returned to Mrs Lowry's property and waited on the path that separated her from the vandalising botanist next door. I had armed my self with a torch and a camera plus a few back up plans. The botanist was quite a large man and I wanted to ensure I remained safe. Sure enough, just after the lights went out in Mrs Lowry's room at nine o'clock, the evil neighbour quietly exited his back door and made his way across onto Mrs Lowry's garden. After a short pause to consider his next actions, he began stamping on the newly repaired Escallonia saplings. Why he had specifically targets the hedge when the whole garden had been landscaped bewildered me. I eventually decided he was just crazy and that was that.

Suddenly the garden was lit up as I clicked away with my camera, its flash light glaring up through the garden and capturing the image of the botanist in his strange activities. In shock he looked up and then began to run towards me, shouting threateningly as he did so. I stood my ground and continued to take photographs, safe in the knowledge that no harm would befall me. Growling like a dog the botanist reached the path on which I stood, little me alone – he thought. He came to a halt in front of me and demanded I hand over the camera. Of course I refused and could not help but grin as he raised his right hand ready to strike me. Then he suddenly noticed Bob, Spike and Trev looming out of the darkness behind me. Within seconds the botanist was restrained none too gently on the ground and the police called for.

By this time Mrs Lowry was awake and leaned out of her bedroom window to see what all the commotion was about. I took some delight as I informed her of what had been happening and that I had photographs to prove it. Her next words were not what one would have expected from a lady of good up bringing and standing in the community. And what she threatened to do to the botanist cannot be repeated here out of simple decency.

The police finally arrived and hauled off the mad botanist. This was of course some years ago when we still had a police force, and the botanist was arrested. I treated Bob, Spike and Trev to a few pints of beer in gratitude for their assistance and at last I considered the episode closed. However three days later I received a pleasant surprise in the post. Mrs Lowry had written a letter expressing her guilt for blaming us for the state of her garden and apologised profusely. She had also enclosed in the letter a large cheque, to cover the extra work we had preformed and as a thank you for our services. I shared the reward with the others later, but at that time I remember feeling like James Bond who had finally defeated the evil botanist and his dastardly plans. It came to light that the botanist wished to purchase that section of Mrs Lowry's garden in order to extend his own. I think she would have happily sold it to him if he had only asked. The garden was large and she was old, but he chose intimidation instead. And then he met us.

I have many memories from my years as a mobile gardener come landscaper. Most were filled with pleasure, some were not. I met lots of very interesting people and had the pleasure of working in some very beautiful locations and gardens. I had the delight of working with some characters who will remain in my memories until I eventually die and decompose and thus the course of nature will continue. The person who worked for me over the longest period was Bob. My recollections of Bob centre on his humour and wit, his ability to discover mirth in what ever chore we faced, and what every scrape I found myself in.

In Trev I found strength and a willingness to push himself against any task that faced him, he accepted a challenge as many of us more sensible folk will accept an offered beer. Spike was something different all together. A young man with fondness of all things black, a Goth in fact but with a gentle trait in his personality that belied his true personality. Spike was a helpful and caring young man who readily responded to the difficulties of others, ever ready to help the older

customer with that little thought or assistance that went
way beyond the content of his employment.

And of course I had my memories of those
unforgettable customers. There was Mr Smith who
craved company and was willing to undergo any amount
horticultural surgery in order to talk to someone. There
was the doctor's mother who always had a list of chores
that required my attention, especially at times when I
was very busy. She could never understand that I had
other customers who were waiting for me and I did
indeed have a time table to keep to. Eventually she
began to call me the *Next week man* as I was always
telling her I would try and do a particular task next
week when I called round again. It did not occur to her
to book in the extra work and thus ensure the job would
be done. Instead she preferred the spontaneous method,
the *do it right now* technique. However it must be said
that the doctor's mother was a lovely person and
forcefully encouraged her group of church goers and
neighbours to take on our services, resulting in a large
clientele in her immediate vicinity.

Mrs Wain repeatedly comes to mind, a
thoughtful woman who recognised my horticultural
failing and took it upon herself to teach me in the

exulted art of distinguishing between the valued flower and the hated weed. I repeat her wise words of wisdom, "If it comes out of the ground easily, it is most likely something that should remain in the flower bed."

Another customer who I have vivid flashbacks to is Mrs Hogh and her poor deceased husband. Thanks to her I am now a keen sailor or boating person, which ever title fits. I have owned boats ever since taking one in lieu of payment and still have one to this day. However that is another story and will be told *A Fly in the Boat*, if I ever finish it.

I have seen few of my former customers since I eventually sold the business of Green Fingers. I would love to meet some of them again and attempt to discover exactly what they really thought of my horticultural skills, or lack of depending how one appraised my work.

Mr Music is one particular customer I would love to become reacquainted with. However the likelihood of that is almost as likely as meeting Mr Hogh, or Mrs Wain or even the adulterer who spent time with his secretary instead of tending his new garden as he had promised his wife. Those memories of my time with Green Fingers occasionally spring to mind. Some very pleasant and filled with happiness, others I would rather forget.

Regretfully after more than a decade of imitating a gardener I suddenly developed acute hay fever. It seemed that over night my eyes grew red and itchy, my nose could have run a marathon and the sound of my breathing resembled a blacksmiths bellows with a hole in it. I tried hiring an extra hand to help cover the work I could no longer do, but that idea failed as I discovered a hired employee will never work as hard as a business owner. My dear wife even stepped in to help but after struggling for six months I decided to sell the business. This was a huge wrench for me as I had to let go Bob, Trev and Spike, all of whom had become close friends. I sold the business as a going concern, in the hope that the new owner would continue to look after and care for all my hard earned customers. Alas this was not to be; instead the new owner soon showed he knew even less about horticulture that I did when I initially began the business with my chain smoking, tea drinking partner. If the new owner had only listened to his wife, the firm of Green Fingers may still have been thriving today. His wife had a sound knowledge of plants and assorted green stuff, she also understood charging rates and how to estimate any prospective future work. Unfortunately her husband and would be business man did not. I believe the business I had given birth to and raised from the soil collapsed some months later.

So my time amputating branches, massacring brambles, beheading lawns of grass and ripping weeds from their comfortable beds came to an end. I was of course very sad to leave my customers and all the friends I had made during my adventures as a mobile landscape and maintenance gardener. However as my old works van loaded with my cherished gardening equipment drove off into the sunset, I shed a little tear and moved on to bigger adventures. My time as a gardener had finally spaded away.

Weeded!

www.ingramcontent.com/pod-product-compliance
Lightning Source LLC
Chambersburg PA
CBHW060230050426
42448CB00009B/1376